# CAREER CHOICES
# FOR UNDERGRADUATES
# CONSIDERING
# LAW

# CAREER CHOICES FOR THE 90's

## FOR STUDENTS OF

# LAW

WALKER AND COMPANY

NEW YORK

Copyright © 1990 by Walker Publishing Company, Inc.

First published in the United States of America in 1990
by Walker Publishing Company, Inc.

Published simultaneously in Canada by Thomas Allen & Son
Canada, Limited, Markham, Ontario

Library of Congress Cataloging-in-Publication Data
Career choices for undergraduates considering law / by Career
Associates.
        p.   cm.
Includes bibliographical references.
ISBN 0-8027-7335-4
1. Law—Vocational guidance—United States.  I. Career
Associates.
        KF297.C33    1990
340'.023'73—dc20              89-70479
                CIP

Printed in the United States of America

2 4 6 8 10 9 7 5 3 1

# CONTENTS

*What's in this book for you?*

# WHAT'S IN THIS BOOK FOR YOU?

With the 1990s in full force and the year 2000—the new millenium!—no longer a distant specter, it's more important than ever to look closely at the changes in different industries. Industries and, consequently, a student's career choices have changed dramatically in the last decade. This book is designed to give you the latest information on a range of different career possibilities.

Recent college graduates, no matter what their major has been, too often discover that there is a dismaying gap between their knowledge and planning and the reality of an actual career. Possibly even more unfortunate is the existence of potentially satisfying careers that graduates do not even know about. Although advice from campus vocational counselors, family, friends, and fellow students can be extremely helpful, there is no substitute for a structured exploration of the various alternatives open to graduates.

The Career Choices Series was created to provide you with the means to conduct such an exploration. It gives you specific, up-to-date information about the entry-level job opportunities in a variety of industries relevant to your degree and highlights opportunities that might otherwise be overlooked. Through its many special features—such as sections on internships, qualifications, and working conditions—the Career Choices Series can help you find out where your interests and abilities lie in order to point your search for an entry-level job in a productive direction. This book cannot find you a job—only you can provide the hard work, persistence, and ingenuity that that requires—but it can save you valuable time and energy. By helping you to narrow the range of your search to careers that are truly suitable for you, this book can help make hunting for a job an exciting adventure rather than a dreary—and sometimes frightening—chore.

The book's easy-to-use format combines general information about each of the industries covered with the hard facts that job-hunters must have. An overall explanation of each industry is followed by authoritative material on the job outlook for entry-level candidates, the competition for the openings that exist, and the new opportunities that may arise from such factors as expansion and technological development. There is a listing of employers by type and by geographic location and a sampling of leading companies by name—by no means all, but enough to give you a good idea of who the employers are.

Many young people are interested in being an entrepreneur and you'll find a section showing examples of people who have succeeded as entrepreneurs in the different industries. There's also a discussion of "intrapreneurship"—how you can be an entrepreneur with a large company.

The section on how to break into the field is not general how-to-get-a-job advice, but rather zeroes in on ways of getting a foot in the door of a particular industry.

You will find the next section, a description of the major functional areas within each industry, especially valuable in making your initial job choice. For example, communications majors aiming for magazine work can evaluate the editorial end, advertising space sales, circulation, or production. Those interested in accounting are shown the differences between management, government, and public accounting. Which of the various areas described offers you the best chance of an entry-level job? What career paths are likely to follow from that position? Will they help you reach your ultimate career goal? The sooner you have a basis to make the decision, the better prepared you can be.

For every industry treated and for the major functional areas within that industry, you'll learn what your duties—both basic and more challenging—are likely to be, what hours you'll work, what your work environment will be, and what range of salary to expect*. What personal and professional qualifications must you have? How can you move up—and to what? This book tells you.

---

*Salary figures given are the latest available as the book goes to press.

You'll learn how it is possible to overcome the apparent contradiction of the truism, "To get experience you have to have experience." The kinds of extracurricular activities and work experience—summer and/or part-time—that can help you get and perform a job in your chosen area are listed. Internships are another way to get over that hurdle, and specific information is included for each industry.

You'll find a list of the books and periodicals you should read to keep up with the latest trends in an industry you are considering, and the names and addresses of professional associations that can be helpful to you—through student chapters, open meetings, and printed information. Finally, interviews with professionals in each field bring you the experiences of people who are actually working in the kinds of jobs you may be aiming for.

Although your entry-level job neither guarantees nor locks you into a lifelong career path, the more you know about what is open to you, the better chance you'll have for a rewarding work future. The information in these pages will not only give you a realistic basis for a good start, it will help you immeasurably in deciding what to explore further on your own. So good reading, good hunting, good luck, and the best of good beginnings.

# ACKNOWLEDGMENTS

Without the excellent efforts of Lynn Stephens Strudler, Assistant Dean of the New York University School of Law Placement Office, this book could not have been written. Special thanks also go to the writers and interviewers, who took time from their duties as law placement officers to gather information, conduct the interviews, and write the chapters that are contained in this book. For his contribution to the organization of the book (and for putting us in touch with Lynn Strudler) thanks are offered to Michael Magness.

# CORPORATE PRACTICE

**A**ttorneys who work for corporations may wear almost as many hats as their counterparts in private practice. Depending on the size and major business of a corporation, the corporate attorney could be a generalist, coordinating the activities of in-house and outside specialists in many areas of law, or might spend his or her entire career practicing in a highly specialized area of the law.

Areas of specialization for corporate attorneys include antitrust law, consumer issues, environmental/energy issues, government contracts, government relations, insurance, intellectual property/computers, international law, litigation, patent law, personnel/labor relations, product liability, real estate, securities and finance, or tax.

In addition to these categories, the *Law and Business Directory of Corporate Counsel* lists 140 additional areas of specialty practiced by corporation lawyers.

Whether a generalist or a specialist, the corporate attorney does a lot of business planning with the employer. This is different from the practice of a private law firm, where the emphasis is on solving legal problems. The corporate attorney attempts to help the employer plan the affairs of the company so that problems do not arise and the goals of the corporation are achieved in a lawful manner.

The numbers and kinds of opportunities with corporations will vary directly with economic and business trends. Companies dealing with computers and software, for example, should be expanding and hiring attorneys, but the intense competition in this field could mean that opportunities with a specific company would decline as its competitors take over a larger share of the market. Similar fluctuations could occur in fields such as oil and gas exploration and production and other energy-related businesses that are subject to world market conditions.

The trend toward mergers and acquisitions in the business world certainly has increased the visibility and importance of in-house counsel. That trend shows no sign of abating; in fact, the situation promises to grow more complex, as more foreign-owned conglomerates join in the takeover sweepstakes. Corporations that do a lot of business overseas may provide some opportunities for international work, although such positions are likely to go to more senior staff members.

Most large corporations do not require specific undergraduate or law school curricula from applicants to their law departments. However, in many cases a business degree or some business background is helpful. Depending on the business of the corporation or the concerns of a specific division in a large law department, a technical undergraduate degree may be required. These would typically include the various areas of engineering or science, and are especially important for an attorney who will be involved in patent law.

## JOB OUTLOOK

**JOB OPENINGS WILL GROW:** Faster than average

**COMPETITION FOR JOBS:** Strong

Although there is a great deal of competition for all law-related jobs, there is probably slightly less competition for positions with corporations than for comparable jobs with private law firms. This is largely due to continuing misconceptions about the nature of corporate jobs and the levels of compensation offered.

**NEW JOB OPPORTUNITIES:** Generally speaking, the outlook for job opportunities with corporations is excellent. Corporations have traditionally depended on private corporate law firms to handle their legal affairs. If they had an in-house attorney, he or she usually did little except coordinate matters being handled by outside counsel. In recent years, however, many corporations are depending more heavily, and often completely, on inside counsel to handle their legal affairs. The reasons for this trend are largely economic. Fees charged by private firms have become so high that most corporations feel they can save money by having their own attorneys on the payroll. Although economic trends and other influences will cause fluctuations in specific industries, the general outlook should still remain favorable.

## GEOGRAPHIC JOB INDEX

Although there may be locations where specific industries tend to cluster, jobs with corporations can be found in every state. Corporate headquarters tend to be located in major population centers, but there are enough exceptions to provide a wide choice of geographic locations and lifestyles to aspiring corporate attorneys. Many corporations are moving their headquarters and research and development centers to new locations in the sunbelt, so job seekers would be wise to investigate new opportunities in southern and southwestern cities.

## WHO THE EMPLOYERS ARE

Virtually any corporation is a potential employer, and major employers can be found in every type of industry. A list of the corporations that hire attorneys would make a book in itself. The corporations with the largest legal staffs are AT&T (which employs more than 900 attorneys), IBM, and Exxon. Most of these larger employers have lawyers working in offices all over the country, with the largest number, of course, in company headquarters.

## HOW TO BREAK INTO THE FIELD

All large corporate law departments have organized procedures for recruiting, and most will interview at law schools. A few of the larger corporations hire summer clerks or interns and try to hire permanent employees from these programs. Smaller corporations sometimes interview on campus, but will more frequently post notices with law school placement offices or advertise openings. The smaller the law department, the more likely it is that the employer will prefer attorneys with experience. However, there is a definite trend toward hiring new people directly from law schools. Students should be alert for these opportunities, particularly in businesses experiencing rapid growth. Anyone interested in working for a corporation should not wait for announcements of openings, but should do research on possible employers, and contact them directly. Send a résumé and cover letter that includes the reasons for your interest in the firm to the head of the law department. As with small firms in private practice, it is possible that the employer may not recognize the need to add attorneys far enough in advance to plan a recruitment strategy. In these cases, the person who has taken the trouble to seek out the employer is often hired before the position has been brought to the attention of placement offices.

## INTERNATIONAL JOB OPPORTUNITIES

Although most very large corporations have offices overseas, it is unusual for such opportunities to be offered to young attorneys recently out of law school. The exception might be foreign nationals educated in U.S. law schools who want to practice law for an American company in their own countries. With some experience, however, the corporate attorney may have opportunities for travel and long-term assignments in any part of the world where the employer has business interests.

# THE WORK

## QUALIFICATIONS

**PERSONAL:** A logical mind. A high moral character. The ability to get along with and work well with others. Tolerance for the sometimes bothersome bureaucratic procedures that are inherent to corporate practice.

**PROFESSIONAL:** A doctor of jurisprudence (J.D.) degree. A license in the state or states in which you will practice. Any additional degrees or training required to follow a particular specialty, such as technical undergraduate degrees for patent law. A firm grasp of the fundamental principles of the law and professional ethics. Excellent research and writing skills.

## CAREER PATHS

Although it is impossible to generalize about career paths in corporations, many large law departments do have very structured paths which attorneys are expected to follow. This would usually begin with some sort of training program for one or more years during which the attorney has an opportunity to become accustomed to the corporation's business and procedures, and to learn about the various activities of the law department. Work would be done in several areas of law under some supervision. The attorney could then expect to move into a particular area of specialty within the law department and gradually progress to higher levels of responsibility, perhaps including a supervisory position.

In smaller law departments, one might expect a less formal training or introductory period and greater responsibility from the beginning. There would also be less opportunity to move into a higher position in a smaller corporation. Both small and large corporations sometimes offer attorneys the opportunity to move out of the law department and into other areas, such as planning, sales, or management. In such cases the opportunities often depend on the interests and initiative of the attorney.

## JOB RESPONSIBILITIES ♦ ENTRY LEVEL

The beginning attorney's job might resemble an entry job in a large law firm. There will be little or no client contact, and a great deal of research and memo writing, possibly on a very narrow area of the law, or even on one case. However, even in large companies, most corporate jobs involve taking on a great deal of responsibility right away, including client contact as well as whatever research and writing is necessary to handle one's own caseload. Some attorneys with smaller corporations are asked to sink or swim as they are given important cases or negotiations immediately after joining the law department. Whether this is good or bad depends on the personality and confidence of the attorney, but most seem pleased to be trusted with important work without a long training period. Help, if needed, is almost always available from other members of the law department.

## MOVING UP

The opportunities available as attorneys move up in their careers are as varied as the business of the companies who hire attorneys. In large companies, there is usually a structured career path in the various branches of the law department which may culminate in a supervisory position. Or the attorney may venture outside the law department to try a nonlegal position in the corporation, perhaps leading to a position in corporate management. Within the law department, the attorney moving up would probably continue to do the same kinds of work (research, writing, and negotiations) but possibly on more and more important matters, and with more emphasis on working with management on business planning. Also, attorneys at higher levels are more likely to hire and supervise outside counsel when it is considered necessary. This involves not only hiring the law firm and specifying the work to be done, but also carefully examining all billing to be sure the corporation has gotten the services it has been asked to pay for. With law firm fees often in the hundreds of thousands of dollars, hiring and supervising outside help can be a large responsibility.

# ADDITIONAL INFORMATION

## SALARIES

There is a common misconception among law students that salaries at corporations are lower than at private firms. Today, corporations compete with law firms for new attorneys, and their starting salaries are usually—but not always—comparable. Larger employers typically offer the highest salaries, as is the case with law firms, but there are always some notable exceptions in smaller but aggressive corporations trying to attract the best legal talent. According to an annual salary survey conducted by David J. White & Associates, a Chicago-based legal placement firm, in the late 1980s the average starting salary for corporate law positions nationwide was about $32,000, while law firms were paying an average starting salary of just over $35,000. Salaries of course are higher in cities like New York, Boston, and Los Angeles. In many areas of the country, however, starting salaries as low as $20,000 were reported for some corporate slots and some law firm positions.

## WORKING CONDITIONS

HOURS: On the average, most corporate attorneys spend no more than about 45 hours per week at the office, although there may be exceptions based on seasonal rushes in certain businesses, and on other special circumstances, such as mergers and acquisitions. Litigators, in particular, often work very long hours when preparing a case. For the most part, though, corporation attorneys work far fewer hours than those in private practice.

**ENVIRONMENT:** Most corporate attorneys can expect to have a private office, a secretary with word processing equipment, paralegal help, and access to a law library, as well as the usual office support equipment, such as copying machines.

**WORKSTYLE:** The atmosphere in corporate law departments is somewhat less competitive than the atmosphere in most law firms. The emphasis is usually on working together as a team, rather than on competing with each other for recognition and a high number of billable hours. Most corporation lawyers spend a great deal of time on the phone and in meetings with their clients.

**TRAVEL:** Most corporate attorneys travel at least some of the time, but much of this travel is discretionary on the part of the attorney. The attorney's travels may take him or her anywhere the client corporation does business, from Podunk to London.

## INTERNSHIPS

Work experience with any legal employer is valuable, but it is not necessary to have worked for a corporation law department. Indeed, there are not many summer positions in corporate law departments, and it is usually only the large organizations that offer summer clerkships. If a student has determined that a large corporate law department job is desirable, then the summer clerkship is important, as the larger employers do try to hire from their summer programs. Information about these is available from the law placement office. However, smaller organizations hire third year students only, and many large employers will also hire third year students when they have not met their hiring quotas from their summer clerkship programs.

## RECOMMENDED READING

### BOOKS
*Law and Business Directory of Corporate Counsel*, Prentice Hall Law & Business: revised annually

*Standard and Poor's Register of Corporations, Directors and Executives,*
Standard and Poor's: revised annually

**PERIODICALS**

*The American Lawyer* (monthly), Am-Law Publishing Corporation,
205 Lexington Avenue, New York, NY 10016

*The National Law Journal* (weekly), 111 Eighth Avenue, New York,
NY 10011

## PROFESSIONAL ASSOCIATIONS

American Bar Association
Corporation, Banking and Business Law Section
1155 East 60th Street
Chicago, IL 60637

Many state and local bar associations (consult the Yellow Pages for
addresses and phone numbers) have corporate counsel sections, some
of which offer student memberships.

# INTERVIEWS

DEBORAH BELLO-MONACO
MANAGING ATTORNEY
THE PRUDENTIAL INSURANCE COMPANY OF AMERICA
NEWARK, NJ

I began working for the Prudential over 10 years ago. I started as a
part-time law clerk, and became Assistant Counsel on my admission
to the New Jersey bar. As an attorney for the company, I worked in
the Prudential's Reinsurance subsidiary. A few months ago, I became managing attorney for the corporation.

While I was in law school, I clerked for a private law firm, which
gave me a first-hand look at how a private firm operates. Attorneys
at the firm often put in six- or seven-day work weeks. As a "part-

time" clerk, I found myself working 35 hours a week. When the Prudential offered me a starting salary equal to those offered by private firms in New Jersey, I took the job.

Attorneys working in corporate legal departments have a somewhat more normal business day than those working in private firms, but the pace is definitely picking up in corporate law. At the Prudential, more legal work is being done in-house, partly because of the high rates charged by private firms, but more so because the attorneys on staff are of high caliber and know the organization much better than outside counsel.

The Prudential's legal department is expanding, although not as fast as the workload. Our legal department now includes about 200 lawyers—250 if you include the lawyers at Prudential-Bache. The bulk of our department is located at corporate headquarters in Newark, but we also have attorneys at our five regional home offices, a number of subsidiary locations, and numerous realty group offices.

Some of our attorneys specialize in certain areas of the law—such as tax, real estate, insurance, and reinsurance—but a good number do general corporate work as well. This is particularly true for the attorneys in our field offices, who may be called upon to do any legal work that needs to be done at their location.

Because the work in-house has become more demanding over the years, the Prudential law department has changed its hiring policies somewhat. The company doesn't recruit students just out of law school any longer. Our new attorneys usually have two to three years of experience, preferably with a private firm, the government, or another corporation, and they've usually graduated at the top of their class. For some specialties, it helps to have an advanced degree—like an LLM in tax law.

ALAN KATZMAN
STAFF ATTORNEY
ON-LINE SOFTWARE INTERNATIONAL INC.
FORT LEE, NJ

After I graduated from law school in 1984, I joined a small private law firm that specialized in corporate and tax law. I worked as an associate at that firm for about three years, and then I joined the legal department at On-Line Software.

I decided to switch from a private firm to corporate counsel for a number of reasons. First, the idea of representing one client appealed to me. As a staff attorney, I can dedicate myself to protecting the interests of one client. For an attorney at a private firm, this is almost impossible to do. An attorney at a private firm may have 10 to 15 active matters to deal with—from 10 to 15 different clients—at any given time. As an in-house counsel, I may have a number of matters to deal with, but they are all for the same client—On-Line Software.

Another advantage to practicing in-house is that I get to interact with other types of professionals, not just lawyers. Attorneys in private firms usually don't get this experience; they typically deal only with other lawyers. As a result, they aren't exposed to other areas of business. They tend to dwell too much on legal aspects of corporate operations. Being an in-house counsel has helped me develop my business inclinations. It has definitely broadened my spectrum, which can only help me in the long run.

The fact that On-Line Software is a high-technology company also attracted me to the position here. I am greatly interested in the technology areas of the law. Intellectual property is a burgeoning aspect of the law, and as an attorney for a major software company, I'm getting a chance to gain a deep knowledge of it.

That's not to say that I concentrate solely on technology. Our in-house staff at On-Line Software is small—four members. I handle as many different aspects as I did as an associate at a private firm. At any given time, for example, I may be called upon to deal with a personnel matter, provide counsel for contract negotiations, or hammer out the details of an acquisition. Again, though, I am only working for one client. I have also found that, despite a small staff and heavy workload, my hours are more predictable than they were at the private firm.

# THE FEDERAL
# GOVERNMENT

You can make a difference as a lawyer in government service. The federal government employs large numbers of lawyers. Many will remain in government service throughout their entire careers. Some may begin their careers in the public sector, develop expertise in an area of practice, and then move into private practice. Still others, whose career commitments are to private practice or teaching, arrange for a leave of absence to render public service.

What is the attraction of government service? You will find that there are differences between the practice of law in the public sector and in the private sector. The private lawyer has a two-fold role, one as a counselor or adviser, where careful analysis and candor are required; the other as a litigator, where the name of the game is advocacy. In public practice you have the same two roles of counselor and advocate, plus a third role—that of policymaker.

The public sector offers attorneys the chance to participate in and to shape actual policy decisions. The public sector offers lawyers a great deal of responsibility and critical experience, often at a relatively young age. There is no altruistic reason that the government gives more worthwhile experience to less experienced lawyers. The truth is that government agencies typically are short on experienced attorneys and long on responsibility. Young lawyers, perhaps a year or two out of law school, may be sent off to argue a particularly complex motion simply because there isn't anyone else with more experience available. In private or corporate practice, a senior partner or officer will not take the chance of putting an important case in the hands of a junior staffer. If the senior partner or officer doesn't handle the case, he or she will make sure that someone with suitable experience does.

Another positive aspect of public service is that you can find yourself doing things that matter, that lead to better, more accountable government. For instance, attorneys with the Environmental Protection Agency are often involved in cases in which the agency is seeking to uphold the nation's clean air and water laws. Lawyers with the National Labor Relations Board are called upon to protect the rights of employees and labor unions in dealings with employers. The fact that the government is so diverse and has so many interests allows job seekers to explore opportunities in agencies whose interests parallel theirs. That's not to say that jobs are available for the taking, however, competition for jobs in the federal government is usually intense.

The fact that the trend in federal administration is heading away from big government has made competition even tougher in the past few years. Deregulation of many key industries, including the airlines and some energy industries, diminished the need for attorneys at the Federal Trade Commission, whose staffing levels fell throughout the 1980s. Budget caps, cuts, and constraints similarly affected other arms of the federal government. Meanwhile, however, other agencies and bureaus have experienced increases in staffing levels. For example, the number of attorneys working for the Drug Enforcement Agency has risen as the nation tries to solve the seemingly unsolvable drug problem.

Just as there are differences between government agencies and private firms, there are also differences between agencies. In the first place, like all institutions, they are made up of people. Just as law firms differ greatly, depending on the personalities of the partners and what their relationships are, government agencies differ in accordance with their size, their turnover, their mission, and their management styles. Some are very exciting places to work, where morale is high, and great flexibility is allowed—the kind of workplace where new ideas are floating around. Others are very highly pyramided structures with tight chains of command. You will find great variations within agencies, as well as across agencies. Be prepared to seek out the kind of agency in which you can work comfortably and productively.

One thing that is missing in practice in the public sector is a live client. You miss the fun of having a client who is excited and enthusiastic about your work. Your client is the people. Unlike private practice, however, it means that you never really bring a case that you don't believe in. The clients don't bother telling you what they think because they are too far away, and so you decide what is right for your client, the people.

Also, as a general rule, support services—secretaries, photocopying, printing—are not as good as those you would have at your disposal in private practice. You also have the challenge of negotiating your way around and through the levels of bureaucracy inherent in a government agency.

Government agencies also use lawyers to fill many jobs that are not necessarily legal jobs. Lawyers may be preferred because of the excellent training they have received and for their freedom from rigid doctrinal approaches. You can wind up doing all kinds of things of an administrative nature. Of the some 10,000 special agents in the FBI, about 400 are lawyers. Any type of work you'd like to do you can find somewhere in a government agency. You are not limited to arguing cases and advising people on legal points. Lawyers in government, perhaps even more than in the private sector, are running the whole operation. The opportunities are tremendous.

## JOB OUTLOOK

**JOB OPENINGS WILL GROW:** More slowly than average. Budget cuts, mandatory reductions in staffing, and deregulation legislation enacted during the Reagan administration continue to squeeze many federal agencies, and although the trend is reversing, a return to staffing levels of the 1970s seems unlikely for some time. The cuts have reduced lateral transfers within the government, thereby limiting—and in some cases eliminating—employment opportunities for new lawyers. Summer intern positions in many cases are on a volunteer basis only.

**COMPETITION FOR JOBS:** Keen. Staffing levels at the Federal Trade Commission, for instance, declined steadily through the 1980s. Turnover is generally low, and hiring freezes are not unheard of.

## GEOGRAPHIC JOB INDEX

The majority of the legal positions with government agencies are in Washington, DC. To locate federal employers in other cities, consult the local telephone book under U.S. Government. You can identify the regional opportunities with a particular agency by referring to the agency's description in the *United States Government Manual.*

## WHO THE EMPLOYERS ARE

Summer internships and permanent employment opportunties for lawyers are available in all branches of the federal government—executive, legislative, and judicial. The executive branch's departments, such as Justice and Treasury, hire the largest number of new lawyers each year. In addition, more than 55 independent agencies and government corporations hire on a more or less regular basis. The Government Accounting Office, Congressional Budget Office, and various congressional committees are potential employers in the legislative branch. The administrative offices of the U.S. Courts, U.S. Tax Court, U.S. Claims Court, and the Federal Research Center and the Federal Public Defenders Offices offer a variety of opportunities in the judicial branch. Consult the *United States Government Manual* for a complete listing of federal employers.

## HOW TO BREAK INTO THE FIELD

Summer internships and part-time employment during the academic year are two excellent ways to learn about government employment and to demonstrate interest in permanent employment upon graduation. In addition to paid positions, some agencies will employ students under a work-study intern program, by which a law school will grant course credit for the experience. Another alternative is to gain experience as a volunteer. Many agencies prefer to hire new attorneys from their second-year interns.

Some federal government departments and agencies interview on campus, although recruiting visits have been cut back in recent years. Other departments, including the Department of Justice, require than an application be submitted. Candidates in whom there is interest are then asked to come in for an interview at regional offices throughout the country. Your law school placement office can supply more detailed information about federal hiring practices.

Some of the most competitive entry positions are filled through the federal government's honors program. In order to qualify for this program, applicants should be in the top 20 percent of their class. Consideration is also given to an applicant's undergraduate record, law school courses and grades, law review work, moot court participation, law clerk experience, and military service. These criteria, in combination with a personal interview and a review of the applicant's writing sample, are used to make a hiring decision.

# THE WORK

## QUALIFICATIONS

**PERSONAL:** Commitment to public service. Ability to work with little supervision.

**PROFESSIONAL:** J.D. degree from a law school accredited by the American Bar Association. Bar exam taken. Admission to any Bar within one year of employment. Extensive experience/coursework in subject area. Interest in continuing legal education.

## CAREER PATHS

| LEVEL | JOB TITLE | ERIENCE NEEDED |
|-------|-----------|----------------|
| GS-11 | Law clerk (attorney upon admission to Bar) | J.D. degree. Bar exam taken. |
| GS-12 | Attorney | Minimum 1 year experience at GS-11 level |
| GS-13 | Attorney | Minimum 1 year experience at GS-12 level |
| GS-14 | Attorney | Minimum 2 years experience at GS-13 level |
| GS-15 | Supervisory attorney | Selection from attorneys at GS-14 level |

## JOB RESPONSIBILITIES ♦ ENTRY LEVEL

**THE BASICS:** Legal research. Familiarizing yourself with cases and issues. Drafting briefs and memoranda.

**MORE CHALLENGING DUTIES:** Discussing approaches to a case with other attorneys. Taking depositions. Preparing witnesses. Court appearances. Responding to inquiries from other attorneys, government employees, or the public.

## MOVING UP

At least one year of service in grade is necessary to be eligible for promotion. The competence you display in the performance of your duties and the degrees of difficulty and responsibility of the assignments you handle are the primary considerations for promotion. Government attorneys are encouraged to continue their legal education through training offered within their agencies and enrolling in after-hours courses in Washington, DC, or regional area schools.

# DEPARTMENT OF JUSTICE

The U.S. Department of Justice has been described as the largest law firm in the world. The Attorney General is the federal government's chief legal officer, whose client is the U.S. government. The Justice Department has more than 18,000 employees in Washington, and over 5,000 lawyers working in the department's various offices, divisions, bureaus, and boards.

The lawyers of the Department of Justice do not do all or even most of the lawyer's work that is done for the federal government, however. Speaking generally, the function of the Department of Justice is to represent the United States in court. The day-to-day office lawyering of the federal government—negotiating contracts, receiving complaints and settling them, providing government officials with legal advice they require in conducting their operation—is done by lawyers in the operating departments and agencies. This kind of legal service is usually provided by lawyers in the office of the general counsel of a department or agency. When a department or agency is involved in or is contemplating litigation, however, the matter is generally turned over to the Department of Justice.

With several important exceptions, the bulk of the department's litigation work is performed by the 92 U.S. Attorneys and their staffs, who work in specific regions. Their work "on the line" is guided and assisted by the lawyers in the several legal divisions in Washington, DC, who also directly handle special categories or cases in their respective areas of responsibility. The principal exceptions to this general division of function between the Department of Justice attorneys in Washington, DC, and those in the field are found in the antitrust, tax, and civil rights divisions, whose lawyers conduct the bulk of the litigation in their respective areas of responsibility regardless of location.

The variety of work to be done is exemplified by the following descriptions of practice in selected Department of Justice offices and divisions.

## U.S. ATTORNEY'S OFFICES

The U.S. Attorney General's responsibility for the conduct of all litigation affecting the interests of the country is discharged by delegating authority to officers throughout the country to handle such litigation and to appear in the various federal courts as the government's advocates. These field officers are the U.S. Attorneys.

There are 92 U.S. Attorneys stationed throughout the United States and its commonwealths and territories. About 2,000 Assistant U.S. Attorneys assist the U.S. Attorneys in preparing and arguing the vast majority of federal cases. Combined, the offices of the U.S. Attorneys prosecute some 90,000 to 100,000 criminal and civil cases a year, representing hundreds of thousands of hours spent before grand juries, trial and appellate courts, magistrates, and referees. The types of cases in which U.S. Attorneys and their assistants become involved are as diverse as the interests of the United States government.

## ANTITRUST DIVISION

As a prosecutorial agency, the Antitrust Division conducts formal civil investigations and grand jury proceedings, prepares antitrust cases for filing, conducts trials, negotiates consent decrees, and enforces final judgments through civil and criminal contempt prosecutions. The division's competition advocacy program involves formal appearances in federal administrative agency proceedings, development of legislative initiatives to promote deregulation and eliminate unjustifiable exemptions from the antitrust laws, participation on executive branch policy task forces, and publication of statutorily required reports on regulated industry performance. The division also provides advice to other agencies on the competitive implications of proposed transactions requiring federal approval, such as mergers of financial institutions, issuance of federal coal and oil drilling leases, and disposition of surplus government property. Twelve of the division's sections are located in Washington, DC—

appellate, energy, evaluation, foreign commerce, general litigation, intellectual property, policy planning, special litigation, special regulated industries, special trial, transportation, and trial. In addition, the division has field offices located in Atlanta, GA, Chicago, IL, Cleveland, OH, Dallas, TX, New York, NY, Philadelphia, PA, and San Francisco, CA.

## CIVIL DIVISION

Described in simplest terms, the Civil Division is the federal government's lawyer. Its clients include more than 100 federal agencies and commissions, individual federal employees acting in their official capacities, the Congress, and, in some instances, even the federal judiciary. The division's principal objective is to provide effective representation in all the traditional ways of good lawyering. The Civil Division's activities are as broad and diverse as the activities of the federal government itself. Because the departments and agencies of the government engage in numerous commercial ventures similar to those of a modern corporation, such as buying, selling, construction, shipping, production of energy, insurance, and banking, the litigation arising from such activities encompasses the complete spectrum of legal problems encountered by private business enterprises. In addition, the division litigates the highly significant policy issues, often rising to constitutional dimensions, associated with governmental activities. These issues often arise in the context of attacks on the constitutionality or statutory validity of actions or programs of various components of the federal government.

## CIVIL RIGHTS DIVISION

The Civil Rights Division is responsible for enforcing the nation's civil rights laws and executive orders relating to civil rights. The division also enforces laws designed to protect institutionalized persons and federal criminal statutes that prohibit violations of an individual's civil rights and interference with the exercise of other federally protected activities.

The primary work of division attorneys involves litigation and related matters. Except for the criminal enforcement work, where cases are normally tried before jury, the suits filed by the division are in equity (i.e., not seeking damages), and are usually tied before a single judge. Through the injunctive process, the division seeks to put an end to actions that violate civil rights statutes or to institute actions that will rectify violations.

## CRIMINAL DIVISION

The mission of the Criminal Division is to serve the public interest through the development and enforcement of criminal statutes in a vigorous, fair, and effective manner.

The division exercises general supervision over the enforcement of all federal criminal laws, with the exception of those few criminal statutes specifically assigned to the antitrust, civil rights, land and natural resources, or tax divisions. The division's responsibility extends to overseeing criminal matters under more than 900 statutes handled in the field by the 92 U.S. Attorneys in the 50 states and outlying possessions. In addition, the Criminal Division supervises certain civil litigation arising under the federal liquor, narcotics, counterfeiting, gambling, firearms, customs, agriculture, and immigration laws. The division is also responsible for civil litigation resulting from petitions for writs of habeas corpus by members of the armed forces, actions brought by or on behalf of federal prisoners, alleged investigative misconduct, and legal actions related to national security issues.

## LAND AND NATURAL RESOURCES DIVISION

Litigation involving the acquisition, administration, and disposition of public lands and natural resources, the protection and management of Indian rights and property, and in general, the safeguarding and enhancement of the American environment fall within the responsibility of the Land and Natural Resources Division.

## TAX DIVISION

The Tax Division is responsible for representing the United States and its officers in civil and criminal litigation arising under the internal revenue laws, other than trial proceedings in the U.S. Tax Court. While the division's primary client is the Internal Revenue Service, it also represents other federal departments and agencies, as well as federal officials, in their dealings with state and local taxing authorities. The Tax Division provides a young attorney with the opportunity to specialize in both tax law and litigation.

## OFFICE OF THE SOLICITOR GENERAL

The major function of the Office of the Solicitor General is to supervise the handling of government litigation in the Supreme Court. Virtually all such litigation is channeled through the Office of the Solicitor General and is actively supervised by that office. This involves about two-thirds of all the cases the Supreme Court decides on the merits each year. (On the merits cases are those that do not involve procedural matters, but are deliberated on the strength of the factual material presented in trial.)

Specifically, the Solicitor General determines the cases in which Supreme Court review will be sought by the government, and the positions the government will take in that court in all the cases in which it is interested. The staff reviews and revises the petitions, briefs, and memorandums filed by the government in its Supreme Court litigation. The Solicitor General personally assigns the oral argument of all government cases, either to himself or herself, to a member of the staff, or to other government attorneys. Most of the government cases in the Supreme Court are argued by the Solicitor General or the staff.

## OFFICE OF LEGISLATIVE AFFAIRS

The Office of Legislative Affairs is assigned the responsibility for coordinating the Justice Department's various contacts with the

Congress. The office exercises general supervision over the department's legislative program and responds to the number of requests and inquiries from congressional committees, individual members, and their staffs.

The functions of the office include maintaining liaison between the department and the Congress, reviewing and submitting department legislative reports, coordinating the preparation of proposed departmental legislation, responding to requests from congressional committees and the Office of Management and Budget for reports on bills and proposed legislation, appearances before congressional committees on justice-related matters, and advising the President on the legal sufficiency of much of the legislation enacted by Congress and presented to the President for approval.

# SECURITIES AND EXCHANGE COMMISSION

The SEC has three major functions—disclosure, regulation, and enforcement—with major issues confronting the commission in each area. As an SEC attorney, you might work in enforcement, corporation finance, corporate regulation, investment management or market regulation, in the Office of General Counsel, or in one of the regional offices in New York, NY, Boston, MA, Atlanta, GA, Chicago, IL, Fort Worth, TX, Denver, CO, Los Angeles, CA, Seattle, WA, or Arlington, VA. Your primary responsibilities would be to ensure compliance with the SEC's disclosure and regulatory policies through one or more of the following activities:

◆ **INVESTIGATING VIOLATIONS OF FEDERAL SECURITIES LAWS (WHICH CAN BE BOTH CIVIL AND CRIMINAL).**

◆ **INSPECTING SELF-REGULATORY SYSTEMS, INCLUDING THE RE-VIEW OF EXISTING LAWS AND REGULATIONS.**

◆ **ANALYZING AND EXAMINING REGISTRATION AND PROXY STATEMENTS, INDENTURES (A FORM OF SECURITY), REPORTS, APPLICATIONS, AND RELATED DOCUMENTS.**

◆ **CONDUCTING HEARINGS OR SOLICITING COMMENTS CONCERNED WITH THE INTRODUCTION OF NEW RULES OR CHANGES IN EXISTING RULES.**

Even as a newly hired lawyer, you may have the opportunity to institute civil suits, litigate suits in the U.S. District Court or before administrative law judges, or prepare briefs and oral arguments for use in appellate litigation.

# FEDERAL TRADE COMMISSION

The Federal Trade Commission employs a mix of strategies to ensure market competition in the consumer interest. As an attorney with the FTC, you might be engaged in litigation before the commission's administrative law judges or in the federal courts to enforce Section 5 of the FTC Act and other antitrust and consumer protection laws. Participate in rule-making proceedings before the presiding officer of the commission to develop rules pursuant to congressional authorization; serve as an advocate before federal, state, and local agencies to encourage adoption of policies promoting competition and consumer interest; assist Congress and its committees in assessing the competitive and consumer implications of its legislation and recommend new legislation; and provide state and local liaison with other enforcement officials to assure an effective program.

The majority of the Bureau of Competition's nearly 200 attorneys work in groups of 15 to 20, with each group being headed by an assistant director. Eight general sections have broad investigative authority and a full range of enforcement responsibilities. Each section tends to focus on one of a number of particular sectors of the economy, and especially those sectors of the economy with the greatest potential to contribute to inflation. A ninth section of attorneys is responsible for assuring industry compliance with competition-related commission orders. Other smaller groups work in areas such as policy planning, evaluation, and premerger notification.

The approximately 150 attorneys who work for the FTC's Bureau of Consumer Protection in Washington are organized in specialized divisions. These divisions do exchange ideas and personnel with one another as well as with other FTC bureaus to find integrated solutions to market problems, and to fulfill the commission's charter to protect the rights of consumers. In addition, the FTC has 150 or so attorneys in regional offices in 10 major cities: Atlanta, Boston, Chicago, Cleveland, Dallas, Denver, Los Angeles, New York, San Francisco, and Seattle. Attorneys in the regional offices typically pursue matters involving a variety of FTC work. Unlike their colleagues at the FTC's Washington, DC, headquarters, attorneys in the regional offices often handle both competition cases and consumer protection cases.

Attorneys in the Office of the General Counsel serve as the commission's chief legal advisers and representatives. They are primarily responsible for many administrative law questions—for example, devising procedures to carry out the commission's mandate and giving advice on difficult legal issues when there is no clear precedent. Much of the work of the office consists of research and legal analysis in response to requests for advice from the commission or a bureau. General counsel attorneys are responsible for many aspects of the commission's relationship with Congress, including preparation of legislative comments and congressional committee testimony. General counsel attorneys also conduct litigation when the commission is a party to federal court action—for example, in support of commission rules and final orders in the Courts of Appeals.

The policy planning staff comprises a small number of attorneys, economists, policy analysts, and specialists in marketing, business, tax, and health policy. Its purpose is to assist the commission in determining where and how FTC resources are best used to serve the public interest. The policy planning staff also works with attorneys and economists in all operating bureaus to develop new initiatives to coordinate FTC activities with other agencies and to ensure that FTC activities will produce net benefits for consumers. Use of various computer-based legal support systems from the commission's Information Services Division provides policy planning and other FTC staff with information capabilities found in few other government agencies.

When the commission issues a complaint, the Office of Administrative Law Judges is responsible for the case until the judge in charge hands down an initial decision. Administrative law judges have been delegated the initial fact-finding function—conducting trials and reviewing evidence in the form of documents and testimony of witnesses. The judges serve under the authority and with the approval of the Office of Personnel Management, holding tenure similar to that of judges in the federal court system. There are opportunities for employment as law clerk to one of these administrative judges.

The Bureau of Economics aids and advises the commission on the economic aspects of its activities and prepares economic information for use by other bureaus. The bureau works with competition and consumer protection attorneys in investigating and evaluating possible law violations. Special economic studies of individual industries and trade practices are also conducted by bureau economists. Bureau reports have often provided the basis for significant legislation by spotlighting uneconomic or otherwise objectionable trade practices.

## FEDERAL RESERVE BOARD

The Legal Division of the Federal Reserve Board includes about three dozen attorneys who are involved in all aspects of the federal regulation of the banking system, including the implementation of monetary policy and the supervision and regulation of banks and bank holding companies. Working as an attorney at the Federal Reserve Board, you would be concerned with questions relating to the fields of commercial, corporate, antitrust, administrative, and banking law.

For example, in support of the board's administration of the Bank Holding Company Act, attorneys analyze proposals for the formation of bank holding companies and the acquisition by bank holding companies of banks and nonbank companies. They are responsible for research analysis and development of necessary revisions to the board's regulations implementing the act as well as monitoring legislative proposals affecting the board's administration of the act. In addition, the legal staff prepares amendments to, and interpretations of other board regulations—such as those dealing with the operation of the nation's payments system and electronic fund transfers, interest rate controls, discounts and advances, and reserve requirements. Other important areas of responsibility include analysis, recommendation, and preparation of testimony relating to proposed legislation in the banking and monetary field; participation in a full range of international banking matters; evaluation of the relationships between banks, savings and loan associations, and securities firms; negotiation and preparation of contracts; interpretation of the Freedom of Information Act, Government in the Sunshine Act, and Privacy Act; and participation at both the trial and appellate levels in litigation affecting the board, which includes both writing briefs and oral arguments.

# ADDITIONAL INFORMATION

## SALARIES

In December 1988, entry-level salaries for government employees were as follows:

| GRADE | ANNUAL SALARY |
|-------|---------------|
| GS-11 | $27,716 |
| GS-12 | $33,218 |
| GS-13 | $39,501 |
| GS-14 | $46,679 |
| GS-15 | $54,907 |
| GS-16 | $64,397 |
| GS-17 | $72,500 |
| GS-18 | $72,500 |

## WORKING CONDITIONS

**HOURS:** Lawyers working in the more visible, highly structured federal departments, such as the Department of Justice and the Securities and Exchange Commission, can expect to work 55–60+ hours per week. Hours may be shorter in other less formal agencies.

**ENVIRONMENT:** For the most part, expect function, not form in government offices. A beginning attorney can expect a small private office and access to support services, although these are generally less abundant than those found in private practice.

**WORKSTYLE:** Depending on your department/agency or job, workstyle varies greatly. For some there will be a majority of research and writing; for others, court appearances from the early stages of a career. Expect to spend a lot of time on the phone and in meetings.

**TRAVEL:** Travel, too, varies greatly, depending on the nature of your work. As a litigator you may travel frequently throughout the United States and even internationally; other jobs require limited (one-day trips to nearby cities) or no travel.

## INTERNSHIPS

Some federal agencies offer internships to students on a volunteer basis or for academic credit. The same is true of public interest organizations in the field of one's interests, such as the Center for Law and Social Policy and the National Wildlife Federation. Consult the career center on your campus for information about internships.

You may also learn about how the government works by serving as a legislative aide to a congressional representative or senator. Inquire about opportunities at your legislator's office.

## RECOMMENDED READING

### BOOKS

*The Almanac of American Politics*, by Michael Barone and Grand Ujifusa, National Journal: revised biannually

*The Congressional Directory*, U.S. Government Printing Office: revised annually

*Congressional Staff Directory*, Congressional Quarterly, Inc.: revised annually

*NALP Employment Opportunity Survey of Government Agencies*, Marilyn B. Norton, ed., National Association for Law Placement: revised annually

*Summer Legal Employment Guide*, by the editors of the National and Federal Legal Employment Report, American Bar Association: revised annually

*United States Government Manual*, U.S. Government Printing Office: revised annually

*Washington Staff Directory*, Congressional Quarterly, Inc.: revised annually

*The Washington Want Ads: A Guide to Legal Careers in the Federal Government*, Moira K. Griffin, ed., American Bar Association: revised annually

## PROFESSIONAL ASSOCIATIONS

The Federal Bar Association
1815 H Street, N.W.
Washington, DC 20006

# INTERVIEWS

### SENIOR TRIAL ATTORNEY
### FEDERAL TRADE COMMISSION
### WASHINGTON, DC

I knew that I wanted to be an attorney from age zero. When I graduated from law school I wanted to do antitrust litigation. I had written a paper on antitrust for an administrative law course I was taking (antitrust was not being taught as a separate subject at that time), and I knew that was how I wanted to spend my career. I went to Washington, interviewed with the Federal Trade Commission, and knew that that had to be it. I was hired from a pool of 1800 applicants for one of 30 available positions. I joined the trial staff in the Bureau of Litigation, planning to stay only three or four years, after which I planned to go on to California and practice.

It never happened, because I have had a very exciting career right here. I have always had a lot of cases. I've traveled—I've seen the entire United States under the auspices of the Federal Trade Commission. I've chased witnesses and had hearings all over the country. We have our own administrative law office and judges. We hold hearings where the witnesses are. We don't work in district court.

Sometimes it can be too much travel, however, especially if you have a family. I didn't marry until I was 35, and when my daughters were quite little, I got involved with a land fraud case that kept me on the road 40 percent of the time, away from the kids and my wife. It was rough for me and it was rougher on my wife. Right now I have the feeling I don't want to travel for another hundred years.

It is a fabulous life. You never get rich, but you earn a good living. Right now I am a senior trial attorney. You progress from less responsible cases, less difficult cases, into the most involved ones. You start out as a bag man to somebody else and then as quickly as possible you get your own cases. The first time they threw me into trial, they sent me to Los Angeles and I didn't even know what a courtroom looked like. I decided to remain with the FTC because while my contemporaries were still carrying bags at law firms, I was trying my own cases. I was arguing cases on appeal. It was very thrilling.

For 25 years I worked 50 to 60 hours a week. With the current administration's policy of deregulation, there is far less action, and I generally work a 40-hour week when I am in Washington, DC. A few years ago there was a call from the local U.S. Attorney's office for trial people to help in district court. Because there was so little work at the FTC, I was able to volunteer. For six months I was a criminal prosecutor.

While the work day is shorter now in Washington, however, on the road, it's still a seven-day-a-week job, anywhere from eight in the morning until midnight. There is no time for anything else.

I have consciously not gotten involved in outside activities. For example, my wife is president of our synagogue, and I would like to be active because they need all kinds of assistance, but I won't commit myself because I know that the minute I sign up I'll be sent on the road and I won't be able to carry out the commitment. So, I don't. I have a greenhouse that I work in around my house, and that's my outside activity.

In this line of work, there is no typical day. It depends on what is on your schedule that day. You could be writing letters for three months or you could be on the road for three weeks. You could be writing briefs, you could be writing memos, you could be arguing with your boss.

Some years back I spent four or five years as an administrator, a deputy assistant director. I supervised all sorts of people. When Lyndon Johnson decided not to run, however, the political situation changed and I was shifted back to the trial staff.

While I am somewhat optimistic that the commission will become more active again in the future, I do not think it will happen quickly. In addition to the political considerations, there is the new arena of international competition to be considered. There are certain areas where that is going to take precedence over domestic antitrust. I have a friend here at the commission who is 20 years younger than I. He travels regularly to Tokyo and Paris on oil matters. He worked with the Federal Trade Commission and then went over to Commerce, where he developed expertise working in their oil section. The FTC called him back and asked him to do some work for the commission in oil. In the last three or four years I know he's been to each of those cities a number of times. I always ask him if he wants a bag man.

I have enjoyed the excitement of my career at the FTC.


**MICHAEL WISE**
**ATTORNEY ADVISOR**
**FEDERAL TRADE COMMISSION**
**WASHINGTON, DC**

I began my career with the Federal Trade Commission about 11 years ago. Prior to that, I had been an associate with the Washington branch of a Chicago-based law firm for about five years.

I joined the Commission to work on big-case litigation. I was primarily a litigator until about three years ago. The most interesting and best-known case that I was involved in as a litigator was the General Motors-Toyota joint-venture case, which was in the news back in the mid-1980s. Most of my other cases involved smaller mergers litigation—those kinds of cases usually don't show up in the newspapers.

As attorney advisor, I provide confidential policy assistance to one of the FTC's commissioners. I do a first-cut review of cases and decisions that are submitted for the Commissioner's decision, and also draft opinions for the Commissioner.

In many respects, the job is like that of a judicial clerk, although it's less of a library job. The most interesting decisions that we make are about whether to file suit over perceived antitrust or consumer protection violations. Our workload can be characterized as episodic, although we're not part of the legislative cycle. We do, however, deal with Congress, responding to requests for help and attending hearings when necessary.

Things have changed quite a bit at the Federal Trade Commission since I joined the staff in the late 1970s. The major change has been in staffing. Heading into the Bush Administration, we're a little over half the size we were a decade ago. Also, we make much greater use of our statutory authority to go to federal court, and cases that 10 years ago may have been brought before the Commission's own administrative law judges are now being brought before the federal courts.

We still hire new people, but obviously not as many as before. Turnover had been low a few years ago, because the demand for antitrust lawyers was low in the private sector. Activity in that area has picked up recently, and more of our senior people are leaving to go into private practice.

## TRIAL ATTORNEY
## NUCLEAR REGULATORY COMMISSION
## WASHINGTON, DC

I like to think of the steps I've taken in my career as a collection of jigsaw pieces. When you look at the pieces separately, they are all different shapes and sizes. They don't look as though they'd fit together too easily, but then you find that they do indeed link up.

The main piece on which I built my career was a clerkship that I was offered soon after I left law school. I had taken a job with a private firm, but I wasn't there long before the opportunity to clerk for a federal district court presented itself. Needless to say, I took the opportunity immediately.

The two years that I spent clerking helped me in more ways than I imagined it would. First of all, the position itself was fascinating. I wasn't just reading about what happens in the highest courts of the land, I was a part of it.

The competition for federal clerkships is intense—few positions are offered considering the volume of applicants. The bright side is that if you are lucky enough to be selected, you generally don't have any trouble making your next career move. Clerks for federal judges are highly recruited by both the private sector and by the government.

A few months before my clerkship expired, I started receiving recruitment letters from various employers. The one from the Nuclear Regulatory Commission intrigued me most. That was because of another of my jigsaw pieces. As an undergraduate, I had taken a number of engineering courses. The NRC didn't recruit me for my engineering knowledge, of course, but my interest in the field led me to take a position with the agency.

I do a lot of high-tech litigation for the commission, mostly involving the operation of commercial power plants. The workload is hefty, but not overwhelming. I find that I can usually take care of business within a reasonable number of hours every week. Even so, you can never tell when you're going to be on a plane to pursue a new case.

I'm very happy with what I'm doing at the NRC. I know I could make more money in private practice, but for now I plan to stay here. I do know one thing, however—I'm still working on completing my jigsaw puzzle.

# JUDICIAL CLERKSHIPS

Judicial clerkships represent a unique opportunity for new law school graduates to spend an additional year or two learning the law and the judicial process from an expert or scholar, the judge. A clerkship is a mutually beneficial arrangement. The clerk has the opportunity to work one-to-one with and to learn from this scholar, and at the same time to refine basic legal skills. The judge has an eager, bright, articulate new graduate who not only handles the time-consuming job of researching points of law and writing the findings into memorandums, but who is able to discuss the issues, act as a sounding board, and play devil's advocate. At its best, a clerkship provides the opportunity to work directly with, study with, and reason with the judge, and to learn the thinking and rationale behind some very difficult decisions. It is an opportunity for a new attorney to get the best possible postgraduate training. Many believe that there is no greater learning experience and no better way to begin a legal career.

The attractiveness of a judicial clerkship as a solid first step into the legal profession has not been lost on law school graduates. The proportion of graduates who are turning to clerkships as their first job experience has increased significantly over the years. In the mid-1970s, fewer than 9 percent of graduating law students became judicial clerks; by the late 1980s, nearly 13 percent of law school grads decided to begin their careers by clerking.

The increased popularity of clerkships means, of course, that the competition for openings is greater than ever. This is particularly true for clerkships at the federal court level. Although competition varies somewhat by region, for federal clerkships hundreds of applications are received for a handful of openings. Despite the long odds, inquiries are worth making. A federal clerkship is certainly a door opener for other opportunities down the road.

Competition for state and county clerkships is generally less intense, although in some regions it can be nearly as formidable as for federal positions. The number of clerkships available depends on the budgets of state and local judicial systems. In some areas, clerks are pooled among several judges, and in other districts some judges must make do without clerks.

The duties of a judicial clerk vary according to the type of court (appellate or trial) and its jurisdiction (federal or state). The raison d'être of each is different, the types of cases handled are different, and, therefore, the clerk's job opportunities are different. Simply stated, trial courts decide issues of fact and law, and appellate courts review the decisions of the trial courts, with the power to affirm, reverse, or modify.

Although all judicial clerks research issues, prepare memorandums on points of law, and discuss opinions with the judges, appellate clerks do a great deal more "academic" work—reviewing the proceedings of a lower court, studying that court's rationale, researching potentially related ideas, analyzing precedent, and discussing possible resolutions of the issue. The appellate court clerk's work is more solitary. The trial court clerk spends a good deal of time interacting with other people—attorneys, judges, other clerks, and the press. As a result, trial clerks have the opportunity to develop important professional contacts. The key differentiation, however, results from the difference in court function. That is, trial court clerks may assist the judge in finding the facts, whereas appellate clerks are bound by the facts. Appellate clerks then are limited in their research to whether the law has been properly applied or whether correct procedures have been followed. In career terms, the appellate clerk is not hindered by the solitary nature of the work; in fact, appellate clerkships are quite prestigious, and are often filled by persons with previous clerkship experience.

## FEDERAL COURT CLERKSHIPS

A position with the U.S. Supreme Court, the highest court in the land, is the most prestigious clerkship and requires impeccable credentials. It is necessary to graduate at the top of your class from one of the nation's outstanding law schools and then to spend a year or two clerking at a lower federal court in order to be considered for these clerkships. The duties of Supreme Court clerks include, but are not limited to, the preparation of memorandums on petitions requesting Court review of lower court decisions, assisting with opinions, preparing "bench memos" summarizing cases before argument, and preparing speeches for the justice.

At the federal appeals level, the United States is divided into 12 geographic areas, or circuits. Each state and the District of Columbia is included in one of these 12 circuits. U.S. Court of Appeals clerks screen cases filed for appeal. Because they deal with a large volume of cases daily, they must quickly acquaint themselves with the facts, check the accuracy of the cases cited, analyze the issues, suggest a line of questioning for oral argument (oral presentation of the merits of the case), and generally brief the judge on the essentials. At that point, a decision is made to dispose of the case or to assign it for oral argument at a later time. After the oral argument, the clerk confers with the judge and then prepares a memo for the judge to use in drafting the opinion. When appeals come in from the district courts, they are heard by three-judge panels that may convene in different cities. It is therefore possible that the Court of Appeals clerk will be spending a week per month in another city, and will have the opportunity to work with other judges and to observe some exceptionally good attorneys at work. A special advantage of clerking on an appeals court is that it gives you a greater sense of the entire judicial process. Not only are you forced to learn the appeals process, but as part of your responsibilities you must become familiar with the pleadings of the trial court.

At the federal trial level, 91 courts in the 50 states (including the District of Columbia and Puerto Rico) are known as U.S. District Courts. In U.S. District Courts, approximately half the clerk's time is spent doing legal research, writing memorandums, and drafting opinions on cases the judge has under submission. The remainder of the clerk's time is spent answering questions from the public and the press, responding to routine correspondence, and perhaps handling administrative matters. One reason why these clerkships are very appealing is that clerks on these trial courts have the opportunity to see both federal and state litigation.

## STATE COURT CLERKSHIPS

The state court systems vary substantially, and therefore it is difficult to generalize about organization. The state court of last resort is often, though not always, called the state supreme court. It may also be called the court of appeals, the supreme judicial court, or the supreme court of appeals. Clerks on the state supreme court study the issues presented by the appeal and prepare memorandums setting out the facts, issues, and a proposed resolution. If a case is argued orally, the clerk generally attends the argument and then confers with the judge to discuss difficult issues. Clerks have the opportunity to participate in important and controversial decisions because this is the state court of last resort.

Clerks on the intermediate courts of appeals, which currently exist in more than 30 states, may have a broader range of experience than their colleagues on the state supreme courts, which handle a lesser volume of cases. The clerk's primary duty is preparing legal memorandums summarizing the facts and issues, analyzing the law on each issue, making recommendations, and perhaps drafting an opinion from a lower court. This is likely to require the checking of citations and possibly doing independent research.

If you are interested in a clerkship with a particular state's trial court system, it is necessary to check with the state court administrative office to determine the organization, number, and location of the state trial courts, and even whether judges on these courts hire law clerks. State trial court clerks research and write memos, draft opinions, and generally confer extensively with the judges. Because the cases being tried originate in these courts, clerks also attend oral arguments, respond to attorneys, and deal with pretrial docket matters and papers that must be filed before a case goes to court. The clerk's duties will to some extent be determined by whether the judge moves from location to location and whether one clerk is serving more than one judge.

## ADDITIONAL CLERKSHIPS

Federal bankruptcy judges and U.S. magistrates hire law clerks, although in the magistrate's office they are often called legal assistants. Presently there is a question about the constitutionality of the bankruptcy courts. Whether bankruptcy clerkships will be available in the future depends on the resolution of this issue. There also are clerkships with special federal courts—the Claims Court, the Tax Court, and the Court of International Trade. For a position on these courts, outstanding performance in work related to the specialty of the court may be more important than overall academic performance. Such experience may be gained through an internship with a law firm practicing in the specialty area, acting as research assistant to a law professor in the specialty area, excellent grades in courses in the area, or special undergraduate training, such as accounting for work on the Tax Court.

Some staff attorney positions available with appellate courts, as opposed to clerkships with individual judges, are of limited duration. They are similar to clerkships in scope of work. There are also motions clerks, who work on litigation papers that come before the court to which they are assigned, and *pro se* clerks, who advise individuals who are representing themselves, on many federal courts. Some state courts hire "pool" clerks to serve the entire court. These clerkships usually are not as comparative as other clerkships, but they are nonetheless valuable learning experiences.

The duties of judicial clerks are affected by the personality and working style of the individual judge. Some judges, after discussion of the case, allow clerks to draft opinions, others refuse to have clerks involved in the opinion writing. Some judges repeatedly use clerks as a sounding board, listen carefully to the clerks' ideas, and treat the clerks as partners. Others are more restrained in their use of clerks and prefer less involvement. Some judges work long hours and on weekends, others maintain a more regular schedule. Judges on some courts, particularly state trial courts, may have a preference for a particular type of case or may be assigned only to a particular area, and so clerking may mean exposure to only one area of the law.

Many judges expect clerks to perform functions unrelated to the business of the court—driving them to appointments, jogging with them, or having dinner together every Tuesday evening. Others, who have a different style, never ask or expect a clerk to be other than a judicial clerk. The way you, the clerk, spend your time will be determined not only by the type of jurisdiction of the court, but by the personality and working style of the judge. Consequently, it is absolutely essential to know as much as possible about a judge before deciding whether you would profit from and enjoy being his or her alter ego. The judge's political philosophy is important to understand and can be ascertained from published opinions, but more important is a knowledge of personal idiosyncracies and work expectations. To a great extent the success of your clerkship may depend on complementary personalities and working styles. In looking for a judicial clerkship, do not underestimate the importance of this fact. There are brilliant, well-respected judges who are excellent to clerk for, and brilliant, well-respected judges who are very difficult to clerk for.

# ADDITIONAL INFORMATION

## THE BENEFITS OF CLERKING

A judicial clerkship is of immeasurable value for a variety of reasons. The clerkship does the following:

**SHARPENS ANALYTIC SKILLS:** The issues dealt with often have major social and political significance, as well as presenting complex legal questions. The work forces you to stretch yourself, and to perfect critical thinking skills.

**STRENGTHENS WRITING SKILLS:** Most law clerks spend over half their time researching and writing. You learn quickly that for a memo to be serviceable it must be well-organized, succinctly written, and grammatically correct, in addition to being thorough and accurate.

**PROVIDES AN UNDERSTANDING OF THE LAW UNOBTAINABLE IN ANY OTHER WAY:** The collaboration with an experienced judge, the debate, and the give-and-take in which a law clerk engages on a daily basis afford a matchless learning experience.

**TEACHES THE ESSENTIALS OF BRIEF WRITING:** Reading hundreds of briefs will undoubtedly increase your ability to distinguish a good brief from a not-so-good one, and to learn from those examples.

**INCREASES UNDERSTANDING OF EFFECTIVE ORAL ADVOCACY SKILLS:** You will hear good and bad oral arguments and will learn which techniques win. If you expect to be a trial lawyer, nothing is more valuable than a clerkship on a trial court.

**IMPROVES MARKETABILITY:** Some clerkships have a greater effect on marketability than others. Federal court clerkships, in addition to being highly competitive, assure potential employers that the law school graduate has received additional training in research and writing under the direct supervision of a highly gifted and experienced practitioner. Because these skills are fundamental to beginning practice in most corporate firms, they are highly marketable to organizations that practice in those courts.

**ALLOWS TIME FOR INVESTIGATING CAREER OPTIONS:** For graduates who are unclear as to the type of legal career they desire, a clerkship not only buys decision-making time without the simultaneous pressures of classroom performance and exams, but offers exposure to a wide range of substantive areas. For those who plan to specialize, a clerkship on the Tax Court, for example, may help to confirm that decision.

**PROVIDES POSSIBLE TEACHING CREDENTIALS:** For those who attend law school hoping to become law school professors, a judicial clerkship has become an increasingly necessary step on the tenure ladder. A judicial clerkship, though not always required, is one of the criteria used in screening teaching applicants, and having survived the competition to be selected as a clerk makes the teaching candidate's life significantly easier.

## QUALIFICATIONS

Judges, like all employers, are seeking the best and the brightest law school graduates. For a federal judicial clerkship it may be necessary to have attended one of the country's prestigious law schools and to rank near the top of the class. Although many judges will consider only those candidates who have held memberships on a law review, they certainly take into account other qualifications. These may include moot court participation (a law school activity that simulates court trials; regional and national competitions are held regularly and participation in these is especially visible and highly regarded), internship experience in a law firm, government agency, or with a judge during law school, or law school clinical experience. Faculty recommendations are also of major significance. Aside from academic credentials, judges have individual preferences. It is not at all unusual for judges to show preference for applicants from their alma mater. At the state level, there is a strong tendency to select clerks from local law schools and to prefer applicants from that state or those who intend to practice there. Judges often mention, in addition, more subjective qualities, such as being articulate and personable, and having a well-developed sense of humor.

## APPLICATION PROCESS

Federal clerkships are more difficult to obtain than state court clerkships. Appellate clerkships are more difficult to secure than trial court clerkships. It is not wise, possible, or practical to apply to all judges. Instead, before applying, evaluate your prospects for obtaining a clerkship as realistically as you can. It may be helpful to discuss options with a faculty mentor or the law school placement director.

Once you have decided to which courts you will apply, carefully study the judges on those courts. Talk with law school deans, faculty, practicing attorneys, and former judicial clerks to learn about the judges. Read whatever you can about them. After determining the judges that interest you, you are ready to begin the application process.

The National Association for Law Placement, an organization of law placement personnel, publishes annually a *Federal and State Judicial Clerkship Directory*. This directory is a compilation of questionnaire responses from federal and state judges which delineate their exact requirements and application process. Law school placement offices may have more in-depth information on qualifications and the application process for judges within their state or general geographic areas.

The first step in the application process is to submit a résumé. This is the single most important document in the process because it is your introduction to the judge. One or more samples of your legal writing may also be required. Some judges prefer to receive writing samples with the résumé; others require samples only from those applicants they decide to interview. Because much of your time as a clerk will be spent writing, these samples are an important aspect of the application process. Your writing sample might be a law review article, a moot court brief, a course paper, or a memorandum written for an employer. Law school transcripts are desired at the outset by some judges, others ask for transcripts only after narrowing down those applicants who will be interviewed.

Recommendations are absolutely crucial to the process. Although the number requested varies, most judges prefer two or more references. Recommendations from faculty members may be preferred to recommendations from employers. Whenever possible, search out professors who are acquainted with both you and the judge to whom you are applying. It can certainly make a difference when the judge knows the recommending professor. For the greatest impact, the reference letters should arrive simultaneously with your application materials. Some law schools have a faculty clerkship committee that screens and recommends applicants. Of course, this can be very beneficial if you are able to obtain the committee's support; however, if you are not one of the few students selected for recommendation, it is still worth applying on your own.

An attempt has been made to standardize the data of application for federal clerkships, and within the past year there have been several changes. Presently the application cutoff date is July 15 during the summer following the second year of law school. This is to allow interviewing during a period when students have no classes and to give judges the benefit of two years of law school grades. As a general rule, however, state court judges do not hire a year in advance of graduation. Thus, the search for a state judicial clerkship could begin the spring of second year and last until after graduation. If you are motivated to clerk, you must assume the responsibility for knowing current application schedules and policy. Check with your law school placement office during the winter of your second year of law school.

Once an interview has been scheduled, prepare thoroughly for this meeting. Learn as much as possible about the judge. Of course, if you researched your initial applications assiduously, you will only have applied to those judges in whom you have a real interest. Read published opinions and determine the judge's philosophical leanings, the type of cases handled, and something about the judge's background. Several publications may assist you in learning about federal judges. For example, the *Second Circuit Redbook* contains photos and biographical sketches of all judges in federal courts in the circuit.

Many states have their own publications on the courts and the justices, and some bar associations also rate judges. The law school placement office may have additional resources. Many placement offices keep anecdotal comments from graduates who have clerked. Talk with faculty and anyone else who may know the judge personally or by reputation. Ask a lot of questions—the more you ask the better prepared you will be for the interview.

Often the judge's present clerk handles the first screening interview to narrow down the pool of applicants. Not only does this save time, but many judges believe that present clerks are better able to analyze the academic and personal qualities of applicants. If the judge requires a two-year commitment, the applicant and the present clerk will be working together, and thus it is sensible for the clerk to have some input. If there is a one-year commitment, the retiring clerk may have to rely on the new, incoming clerk to complete unfinished projects. In both instances the present clerk has a stake in the selection.

When you receive an offer to clerk, you should be ready to accept it immediately. Before you applied, you narrowed down the choices. You researched even further those with whom you accepted an invitation to interview. By the time an offer is made, you will have met the judge and will have had time to learn even more about him or her. You will have spoken with the present clerks and will have some sense of whether you would enjoy such a clerkship. It is improper to play one judge off against another or to expect to buy additional time while you learn of other employment opportunities. Therefore, it is wise to apply to and to accept interviews with only those judges in whom you are genuinely interested.

Although the selection process in some state courts is similar to that just discussed, in other states it is totally different. Clerks may be selected for the court as a whole through a special procedure that could be implemented by the court's administrative office, by a single judge hiring for the court, or by a committee of judges who screen and select all applicants.

Salaries for federal judicial clerks are determined by the Judicial

Salary Preference (JSP). Clerks begin at the JSP-9 or JSP-11 grade. After they have been admitted to the bar and practice for a year, they move up to a JSP-12 grade. In 1988, salaries for federal judicial clerks ranged from $21,804 to $41,105. The 24 clerks who worked for U.S. Supreme Court Justices each earned $31,619.

## CAREER PATHS

From a clerkship new lawyers follow a variety of career paths—they practice with private law firms, begin legal careers with government agencies, work for public interest organizations, or join corporate legal departments. One does not make a career out of a judicial clerkship, although clerks on a lower court, if they have enjoyed their initial clerkship and feel that additional experience will help to increase their marketability, may seek a clerkship with a higher court for a year or two.

A judicial clerkship is one stepping-stone in the path of a legal career, but it is not an end in itself. It is a postgraduate training period that generally provides additional knowledge, skill, self-confidence, and marketability, and it is an excellent beginning for any legal career.

# INTERVIEWS

MONICA BARRETT
CLERK
NEW JERSEY SUPERIOR COURT, APPELLATE DIVISION,
HACKENSACK, NJ

As an undergraduate at Wellesley, I was active in various feminist organizations. After graduation I worked in publishing at Alfred A. Knopf for two years. Because of my attraction to public interest law, especially that concerning women's issues, I applied to the University of Michigan law school. While at Michigan, I taught an undergraduate course on Women and the Law in the Women's Studies Department.

During the summer of my second year of law school, I applied to and interviewed with several judges for clerkship positions. The position I have now, which began the September after graduation, is for one year.

As a law clerk, I have a great opportunity to get a broad view of the judicial system. My work involves mainly research and writing, experience of which you don't get enough in law school. This work is helping me to discipline myself to write clearly and quickly.

In New Jersey, all cases have first right of appeal through the Appellate Division. My job involves reading briefs submitted by both parties in a civil or criminal case and researching the legal issues raised. I then write a legal memorandum, which averages 25 pages, that sums up the laws on the issues and offers a conclusion. This is used as a tool by the judges who sit on the appeals panel. I also have emergent duties one week each month, during which time trial court rulings that require an immediate appeals hearing are handled. That's when I deal most closely with attorneys.

The workload is fairly heavy, usually running 9:00 to 5:30 daily and some weekends. But because the cases are assigned to me weeks in advance, I'm able to organize my time efficiently.

A friend of mine had clerked as a staff attorney for the Michigan Court of Appeals, so I had a good idea of what the job entailed. I think my experience has been somewhat better because I work for one judge and am able to interact directly with her and receive immediate feedback on what I've done.

I will be working as an associate in a law firm here in New Jersey this fall. I'd like to be involved in public interest litigation, particularly women's rights, either on the job or as a pro bono activity.

# POLITICS

D emocratic government favors the political power of lawyers. When the rich, the noble, and the prince are excluded from the government, the lawyers step into their full rights, for they are then the only men both enlightened and skillful, but not of the people, whom the people can choose.

Alexis de Tocqueville
*Democracy in America*

For many years, the advice given law school graduates who had difficulty locating paid employment was, "Run for office!" These words of wisdom were only partially tongue-in-cheek. Lawyers formed a majority of many elected bodies and dominated the political process in the mind of the public. However, in recent years, not only the perception but the reality has begun to change.

Single-issue candidates representing movements that ranged from pro- to anti-abortion, or right-to-work laws and civil rights began to dominate local, state, and national election contests. The U.S. Supreme Court decision in 1977, which allowed lawyers to advertise "routine" legal services, reduced the need for visibility which previously might have been met by an election contest. Changes in state laws also have affected the political track. In the past, most state legislatures met only for a few months every other year. Now, most states require their legislatures to meet annually, and in many states there is no limit on the duration of a session. Today, sessions lasting from January to July are not uncommon. Consequently, it has become virtually impossible for lawyers to maintain their private practices while holding public office.

Any or all of these factors may have contributed to the declining number of lawyers willing to commit themselves to careers as active politicians. Another possible explanation is that the number of lawyers running for office has remained constant, but because of the generally negative public image of the legal profession in the post-Watergate era, they have lost to less "establishment" candidates. Whatever the reasons, statistics demonstrate that something is affecting the percentages of lawyer-legislators.

Between 1966 and 1979, the percentage of lawyers in state legislatures dropped from 26 to 20. The 96th Congress (1980–1981) contained fewer lawyers than any session during the preceding 30 years. The House of Representatives, with 435 members, did not have a majority of lawyers for the first time in three decades. That trend continued through the 1980s, and in the 101st Congress (1989–1990), only 42 percent (184) of House members listed law as their profession. In the Senate, the pattern has been less pronounced. The 95th Congress (1977–1978) included 68 lawyer-senators. That number dropped to a low of 59 for the 97th Congress (1981–1982), but rebounded to 63 for the 101st Congress.

For these reasons, among others, this chapter will focus on lobbying and legislative positions—jobs which lawyers may do that are related to politics, but not necessarily of politics. Positions with trade and professional associations and, more recently, with political action committees, often have appealed to attorneys with a service orientation who did not have the inclination to mount a political campaign. Legislative staff positions served to meet a similar need for lawyers with a great deal of interest in the law-making process who had not yet developed a political constituency that would enable them to run for office successfully.

The number of lawyers occupying salaried positions in these two categories of employers remains relatively small. The 1989 edition of the *Law and Business Directory of Corporate Counsel* lists fewer than 1,000 attorneys working for trade associations nationwide. Although it is difficult to come up with the number of attorneys with legislative staff positions—their numbers generally are masked by an overall figure for government employment—it's safe to say that the number of such positions is limited.

# LOBBYING

Lobbying is an activity that the public commonly associates with lawyers. Not all government relations specialists, as lobbyists are frequently titled, are lawyers. However, many of the functions that this group of specialists performs are most effectively performed by lawyers.

The most frequent employers of full-time lobbyists are corporations, trade and professional associations, and their political action committees (PACs). In addition, the role of law firms as lobbyists, particularly in Washington, DC, is well known. Attorneys who work for public interest advocacy groups, such as Common Cause, the Food Research Action Center, or the National Low Income Housing Center, usually function as lobbyists as well.

Lobbyists are responsible for presenting the positions of the group they represent to legislative and regulatory bodies and government executive departments. They function at all levels of government, so persons seeking positions in this area are well advised to consider positions at the state and local, as well as at the national level. Their presentations may take the form of testimony before legislative committees, individual meetings with key legislators, or detailed written information about pending bills. Moreover, they must keep upper management informed of legislation that may affect their corporation, or, in the case of associations, elected officials must receive these communications.

In some situations, a lobbyist's role may require that he or she provide written drafts of a statute or rule, suitable for incorporation into legislation. Legal training clearly is helpful for this activity, as well as for those described above. Given the complexity of our system of government and its legislative processes, however, it is not unusual to find counsel to larger organizations doing the drafting, but relying upon a government relations staff to do the presenting.

## JOB OUTLOOK

**JOB OPENINGS WILL GROW:** About as fast as average

**COMPETITION FOR JOBS:** Strong

**NEW JOB OPPORTUNITIES:** Major corporations will continue to expand their lobbying departments to enable them to meet the demands of strong public interest in areas such as product safety, environmental protection, and protection of revenues from state and local level taxation. The same trends are reflected in the government affairs staffing of business and trade associations.

Staffing in trade and professional associations tend to be more stable because these organizations are made up of individual members, whose numbers typically are more or less fixed. The number of industry and trade association lobbyists decreased sharply during the Reagan Administration, primarily because that administration's commitment to the deregulation of industry largely eliminated the need for resident lobbyists. According to surveys by the National Association for Law Placement, in 1978 5.9 percent of all law school graduates joined public interest groups. By the late 1980s, that proportion had dropped to about 3 percent.

Although many trade associations and interest groups expect the commitment to deregulation to continue with the Bush Administration, others foresee the regulation pendulum swinging the other way. Political action committees which grew rapidly in the 1980s, accounted for a higher proportion of lobbyists in the nation's capital, and lobbying efforts on the state and local levels have picked up in the past few years. On balance, then, the outlook for lobbyists is promising, for our form of government virtually mandates participation in the legislative process by interested parties, and lobbyists are the representatives of those parties.

Lobbyists will find other new opportunities in the wake of changes in the political and legislative climate. Public interest lobbyists were a product of the political climate of the 1960s and 1970s. Energy lobbyists followed close behind. As social and economic changes create new areas for government intervention, new job opportunities will evolve. A critical skill for developing a career in this area will be the ability to look ahead on the political road and spot newly evolving areas of concern before the competition becomes too intense.

## GEOGRAPHIC JOB INDEX

Persons serious about working as lobbyists need to be willing to consider living in one of 50 state capitals or Washington, DC. Alternatively, one can consider three other cities where most organizations that employ lobbyists have their headquarters—Chicago, IL, Los Angeles, CA, or New York, NY. If your interests are highly specialized, consider those cities in which the organizations reflecting those interests are concentrated. For example, the mutual funds industry tends to be limited to Boston, MA, New York, NY, and Philadelphia, PA. Depending on your areas of interest and the kind or organization for which you want to work, you may have a great number of geographic choices as a lobbyist. At the same time, you will have to be flexible with respect to both location and job responsibilities when looking for an entry-level position.

## WHO THE EMPLOYERS ARE

TRADE AND PROFESSIONAL ASSOCIATIONS AND LABOR UNIONS employ lobbyists to promote their causes to legislators in Washington, DC, and in state capitals.

CORPORATIONS hire lawyers to handle their relations with government at national, state, and sometimes local levels.

PUBLIC INTEREST ADVOCACY GROUPS need lobbyists with legal training and an interest in their causes, which range from gun control to the Equal Rights Amendment to prison reform.

LAW FIRMS employ lobbyists to represent clients in regulatory matters and legal confrontations with government.

## MAJOR EMPLOYERS

The range of potential employers is vast, with opportunities in almost every area that makes up economic and social America. Business or trade associations range from the enormous National Association of Manufacturers and the American Banking Association in Washington, DC, to the much smaller Credit Union National Association in Madison, WI. Professional associations include the American Medical Association and the American Bar Association, both in Chicago, IL, as well as the various subject matter groups that constitute the Social Science Research Council, New York, NY. Fortune 500 corporations employ lobbyists, and law firms designate partners, and even employ some nonlawyers, who work as lobbyists. Public interest groups and labor unions, ranging from Common Cause in Washington, DC, to the International Ladies' Garment Workers Union in New York, NY, are potential employers. The bibliography at the end of this chapter lists directories that will help identify potential employers.

## HOW TO BREAK INTO THE FIELD

Lobbying is a competitive, results-oriented field, and there is no sure formula for breaking in. One need only look at the career paths of successful lobbyists to see the various courses they have taken. Some have been legislative assistants in state or national bodies. Others have worked as attorneys for government agencies, while still others have had experience in private practice. Many association lobbyists accepted their first job after law school with the organizations for which they now lobby. A large number maintain private practices and divide their time between lobbying and serving private clients.

If you wish to work as a lobbyist in the nonprofit sector, you should make direct application to the executive director or staff director of organizations to which you bring an area of expertise, or in which you have a professional or personal interest. Those who aim for corporate positions should apply (through the usual cover letter, résumé and follow-up phone call) to the head of the government relations departments of corporations they have researched thoroughly. Depending on the corporation, this department may be called by various names, such as regulatory regulations or public or government affairs.

## INTERNATIONAL JOB OPPORTUNITIES

Perhaps inevitably, a sigificant number of those persons employed to lobby at the international level are foreign nationals with preexisting contacts in those countries where they lobby. However, for American citizens who work to develop similar contacts, an increasing number of international opportunities are available. Multinational corporations employ people with backgrounds in government affairs, particularly with organizations that are international in scope, to represent their interests to foreign governments. Some trade and professional associations have international concerns, and the same is true for certain public interest groups. Only significant expertise in your area of interest will make you an attractive candidate to handle the international affairs of such groups.

## THE WORK

Whether one is working for a nonprofit association or a profit-making entity, lobbying often is hectic. The fact that government relations permits high visibility must be weighed against the pressure imposed by the requirements of the job. Lobbyists most often work alone or with limited staff. They must remain in constant communication with their superiors, as well as with legislative bodies, when they are in session. Regulatory commissions and executive departments are constantly active, and impose yet another set of communications necessities.

The realities of a lobbyist's life, more often than not, come down to eating lunch or dinner on the run, trying to grab a moment with a legislator whose vote or opinion is crucial, reviewing and analyzing key legislation, checking amendments to be sure that changes are acceptable, taking apart voting records, and trying to determine support or opposition for an issue before it comes to the floor.

The lobbyist who works at the state level is more often than not engaged in this activity on a part-time basis, making the months when the legislature is in session particularly hectic. Shuttling back and forth between the state capital and the location of your private practice becomes a time-consuming routine, and the toll on personal and leisure time is great. A strong commitment to an issue is necessary to balance the toll of this hard work.

Lobbyists working for associations may find themselves in a situation where they must perform more than one role. Nonprofit organizations with small staffs must rely on their employees to fulfill any number of functions, including membership services, education, convention planning, editorial work, and public relations. If a key piece of legislation comes to the floor at the same time as the organization's annual convention begins, all members of the staff may find themselves under a great deal of stress, but the government relations specialist will be particularly pressured.

Finally, lobbyists must be capable of maintaining their energy and enthusiasm despite changes in the political landscape around them. The nature of the work they do requires that lawyers in this area be particularly competitive, and it follows that they do not like to lose. At the same time, for a lobbyist representing an organization that is identified with liberal or conservative issues, a change in the make-up of the government may make losing inevitable. In order to weather vicissitudes of politic life, you must either enjoy mastery of the process or believe in the cause for which you work.

## QUALIFICATIONS

The qualifications for a lobbyist are almost as diverse as the interests represented. Legal training is of great assistance and, in fact, most lobbyists are lawyers. In addition, the lobbyist's image long has been that of a gregarious, outgoing person who gets along well with almost everyone. Persons in the field have noted several other professional traits that are essential in successful lobbyists.

First, the representative must be informed and articulate on the issues in question. He or she must be able to marshal the facts in support of their client's position, and present them effectively to the relevant legislators or regulators. The lobbyist must have a reputation for integrity, and the expertise that gives rise to credibility. Finally, he or she must understand the process in which they are participating so that they can anticipate the pressures which may be brought to bear upon the individual whose assistance they are seeking.

No particular training or academic credentials will give you these characteristics. A service-oriented attitude helps, particularly for those representatives who work for trade and professional associations, because ultimately those organizations exist to serve their members. All lobbyists must be able to enlist the support of others from time to time, whether they are trying to mount a grass roots campaign or form a legislative coalition. Thus, tact and related people skills may be qualifications that are just as important as the experience that leads to mastery of a substantive area and an understanding of the legislative or administrative process.

## JOB RESPONSIBILITIES ♦ ENTRY LEVEL

Because of the diversity of the areas which lobbyists represent, job responsibilities in entry-level positions vary enormously. Eventually, the lobbyist's responsibility is to bring about government action favorable to the client or, if necessary, to block unfavorable action. Beyond this, the responsibilities of persons working in this area may vary as much as their titles. Lobbyists may be called everything from specialists in Washington activities to legislative counselors, regulatory liaison, public affairs officers, government relations officers, or, simply, lawyers.

Some specialize in information-gathering, and their most important responsibility may be to ensure that their corporation's or association's executives are informed about trends upon which they must act. Others may see their role primarily as legal counseling and may not even wish to be identified as lobbyists. However, their role can easily move beyond advocacy to designing strategy to modify or block legislative or executive action unfavorable to their clients. Finally, others—whether or not they register with the Department of Justice as lobbyists or foreign government representatives—may nonetheless devote their time to influencing the political process directly to bring about their clients' desired results.

However they define their responsibilities, lobbyists are key actors in the process by which issues are defined, factual data is amassed, arguments are prepared and presented, legislation is drafted, and voting coalitions are mobilized. They may participate in every aspect of the process themselves, or rely on their staffs or superiors to discharge some of these duties. Perhaps their most important responsibility is knowing how to orchestrate a process that involves multiple actors so that the results achieved are consistent with their clients' interests.

## MOVING UP

A variety of career options are available to lobbyists. Lobbyists who work for associations tend to have a great deal of visibility. Particularly in organizations with a large membership, they may be required to travel frequently, but travel presents an opportunity for recognition and increases mobility and versatility. Some elect to remain with the organizations with which they started, moving up internally to executive staff positions, or heading up the organization as executive director. Others may choose to move on to larger, more prestigious organizations, where pay and visibility are even greater. Not infrequently, as their work becomes known, they may be hired away by member companies in their group, or to a senior position in government.

Corporate lobbyists are equally mobile. They may move up into executive positions with their corporation, or another engaged in similar business, to a position such as vice president for government affairs, where they would be responsible for directing both Washington, DC (or state capital), and home office activities. They may take their skills to law firms. (Association and public sector lobbyists may also find employment in private practice.) In private practice, lobbyist-lawyers continue lobbying efforts on behalf of private clients of the firm. The most successful will be designated partners, with responsibility for the firm's lobbying efforts.

For those with an entrepreneurial bent it is possible to become self-employed as an independent lobbyist, representing industry groups or other associations on a retainer basis. Some lobbyists, especially those with public sector experience, move back and forth between lobbying and the pursuit of other professional interests.

## SALARIES

Starting salaries can be low in this area, particularly in membership associations, such as trade and professional groups. Entry-level positions pay an average of $22,000 a year, but many pay less than $20,000. For corporate lobbyists, salaries tend to be higher, typically $40,000 or more a year.

For lobbyists in all areas, however, experience pays. Association executives, including counsel and government relations experts, typically earn salaries ranging from $35,000 to $50,000 per year. Some association salaries exceed $100,000 per year in organizations with large memberships and budgets. Experienced corporate lobbyists may also earn $100,000 annually, and those who reach executive levels may earn even more.

## WORKING CONDITIONS

**HOURS:** Hours are long and can be erratic in lobbying, especially when a bill that is crucial to your client is being drafted or considered.

**ENVIRONMENT:** If you are working for a corporation or for a professional or trade association with a large budget, you can expect a private or semiprivate office and adequate support staff. Surroundings will be less comfortable at less well-endowed associations and public interest advocacy groups.

**WORKSTYLE:** Because lobbying is largely presentational, expect to spend a lot of time meeting with people who can help promote your client's interests, either on the phone or in person. Time will also be spent gathering and analyzing the information that is crucial to promoting your client's point of view.

**TRAVEL:** Some lobbyists, especially if they work for nationally visible groups with interests to protect throughout the country, will travel frequently, to speak on their client's behalf or to garner support for their interests. Others, whose client's interests are less broad, will travel infrequently or not at all.

## INTERNSHIPS

Positions as diverse as volunteer jobs with trade or business and professional associations and summer internships with government agencies or legislative bodies may provide useful experience for persons interested in lobbying. Enough lobbyists have been recruited from the private bar that a summer associate's position with a law firm that provides lobbying services may be equally helpful. Public interest organizations are well known for their proclivity to offer permanent positions to those who have worked as interns during their law school summers, but often those internships require that one be able to work as a volunteer.

In short, the kind of clerkship or summer job an aspiring lobbyist selects should be related to the area in which he or she intends to work. If your goal is government relations for a particular industry, check first to see whether any corporations in the industry offer summer positions. If not, the industry's trade association is another alternative. If there still is nothing available, investigate the possibility of an internship with a legislative committee or a congressperson's staff that is actively involved with some aspect of corporate legislation.

Your law school placement office can be helpful in identifying these positions and the proper application processes, as can the directories listed in the "Recommended Reading" section at the end of the chapter.

## LEGISLATIVE POSITIONS

Persons who thrive on fast-paced action, daily contact with the rich and famous, or the sense of power that comes with direct input into the legislative process often will obtain a real sense of fulfillment in legislative staff positions. The structure of available employment with and around the U.S. Congress virtually parallels the jobs that may be found around most state houses. However, most recent law school graduates who have been bitten by the political bug look first to Washington, DC, unless they have developed strong ties to state interests while in law school. Consequently, the material that follows will focus on staff positions with the U.S. Senate and House of Representatives.

About 19,000 people work on Capitol Hill in the direct service of senators and representatives. Another 18,000 to 19,000 work in the legislative branch in such organizations as the General Accounting Office, the Government Printing Office, the Library of Congress, and the Office of Technology Assessment.

Congressional staffers tend to be among the first casualties after any election. Newly elected representatives bring their own staffs with them, and if control of either the House or the Senate changes from one party to the other, even the fairly secure committee staffers find themselves switching from majority to minority status. As a result, the Hill staff is predominantly young, and a tenure of one or two years generally is an acceptable basis, or at least a commonly used one, to be counted among the experienced staffers.

Turnover rates average about 40 percent annually. In other words, 7,600 Hill staffers transfer, quit, or are fired each year. Congress keeps no figures on the total number of lawyers employed on the Hill, but if the 40 percent figure is applied to the 1,700 legislative staff positions classified as "professional," many of which are filled by lawyers, one comes up with a total of 680 available positions each year.

Capitol Hill clearly is a fertile hunting ground for recent law school graduates, even without considering the numerous positions filled by attorneys on the individual staffs of representatives and senators.

Each member of the House of Representatives may employ up to 18 people, at a maximum total expense of about $370,000. There is no limit on the number of employees a senator may have, but the maximum spending allotment for each senator is based on the size of the state he or she represents. Senators from California and New York have the most money to spend, while senators from the least-populated states, Alaska, Wyoming, and Delaware, get the least.

A basic fact of life for the legislative job seeker is that each office operates autonomously in terms of hiring and salaries. Placement offices exist in both the House and Senate, and their addresses are included at the end of this chapter. However, they are largely ineffective for the person seeking any job other than a support position. Law school graduates who aspire to legislative positions must be prepared to deal separately with the administrative assistants in 539 elected representatives' offices (sometimes responsibility for hiring is delegated to an office manager or senior legislative assistant, but you can only find out whether that is the case by being there—and asking!), and with the staff directors of the 37 full committees, 224 subcommittees, and the various joint, ad hoc, and select committees.

## JOB OUTLOOK

**JOB OPENINGS WILL GROW:** Little change.

**COMPETITION FOR JOBS:** Strong.

**NEW JOB OPPORTUNITIES:** New job opportunities arise whenever a special congressional committee or subcommittee is created. Ad hoc committees and select committees also provide fresh opportunities. At the state level, legislative staffs are beginning to expand rapidly, and the alert student of the political process may be able to ride the crest of that expansion. Finally, city council members' staffs offer yet another opportunity for legislative experience. It is one that is frequently overlooked, because attention tends to focus on Washington, DC. However, municipal government is acquiring increased responsibilities in this period of deregulation, and should be investigated as another source of legislative positions.

## GEOGRAPHIC JOB INDEX

The greatest concentration of high-visibility legislative positions is in Washington, DC. However, for the person who wishes to remain closer to home, state capitals and municipal governments offer excellent opportunities. The number of legislative employees in large states like California and New York is comparable to the number in Washington, DC. Moreover, many state legislatures still offer the possibility of part-time professional positions, which is not an option generally available in the nation's capital beyond the internship level. Wherever the aspiring legislative staffer eventually decides to work, opportunities are numerous and frequent for those who are persistent and well prepared.

## WHO THE EMPLOYERS ARE

Employers are elected representatives at the national, state, and local government levels. Access to available opportunities typically is obtained through applications made to congressional administrative assistants, committee staff directors, and their counterparts, who frequently have the same titles, at the state and local level.

## HOW TO BREAK INTO THE FIELD

Anyone looking for a job on the Hill or in a state legislature should do some targeting as a firt step in the job search. Targeting means evaluating one's own interests, skills, and areas of expertise in relation to those of the members of the legislature. If the applicant is a social and economic liberal and the legislator is extremely conservative, the match may be extremely uncomfortable—even if the unlikely occurs and the applicant gets the job. The same principle applies in interviewing with committees. An expert in weapons technology finance will be wasting time interviewing for a position with a committee that specializes in housing.

Yet another factor in planning job search strategy is the home state advantage. Your own representatives will provide a warm welcome. Even if they do not have an available position, they frequently will be a source of useful referrals. In a few cases, individual members of Congress insist on staffing their Washington, DC, offices with residents of their home state, so the applicant's chances are further enhanced. The home state advantage is usually greatest for those who come from states located far from Washington, DC, and which are lightly populated.

Timing also is crucial in finding a permanent position on the Hill. Being in the right place at the right time often produces the job offer. However, a few rules of thumb exist. The greatest turnover in any congressional session occurs during the first 90 days. During that period, many new staffers who arrive with newly elected legislators leave for reasons that include disappointment with the city, disillusionment with their jobs, and simple homesickness.

Beyond this period, most full-time positions open up only when a staff member leaves and, occasionally, when a member changes committee assignments. Being there, then, is a crucial part of the strategy for breaking in.

Finally, campaign work has long been a favored method for making contacts, but there are two inherent difficulties in this method. First, there are no guarantees that the job seeker will have enough visibility in the campaign organization to attract the candidate's attention. Second, even if one has visibility, there may not be enough jobs to go around. Nevertheless, many applicants consider these to be risks worth taking.

The best way to actually find a legislative job is to get out there and do some good old-fashioned networking. Make the rounds to staff directors; use any contacts you have to get in to see them; take people to lunch, invite them to dinner at your house, do whatever it takes to become visible. It is possible to be hired by going through the mass mailing of letters and résumés route, but this is less efficient than simply going out there and letting it be known that you are available, enterprising, and able.

## INTERNATIONAL JOB OPPORTUNITIES

The opportunities for moving from a legislative position to one with an international or intergovernmental organization are extremely limited. Persons seriously committed to careers with international organizations or jobs abroad probably would do better to seek positions with executive departments that have responsibilities in these areas or overseas field staffs.

## THE WORK

Legislative positions offer staffers exciting and demanding work, and an opportunity to influence decisions that will affect the daily lives of their fellow citizens. However, there is one important caveat that must be issued to anyone considering a congressional staff job. Legislative offices are virtual fiefdoms, and any staffer will have to be able to subordinate his or her needs for personal recognition to a responsibility to enhance the reputation of the legislator. This may be true of committee work as well, because committee counsel, staff directors, and professionals all are appointed at the behest of a particular legislator. Some people may find this requirement—that they suppress their identity and ego for the benefit of someone else—particularly onerous. In addition, all novices on the Hill are warned to avoid individual members' offices where turnover is usually high. Certain members of any organization are capable of burning out staff at a rapid rate. The savvy job seeker will avoid their part of the Congress, or at least make sure that it represents no more than a temporary stop.

## QUALIFICATIONS

A demonstrated interest in politics, either through active campaigning, undergraduate major, or research papers and articles, will go a long way in launching a career as a legislative staffer. An area of expertise, especially one that is keyed to the work of a particular committee or that reflects the interests of a particular member's constituency, will also increase your chances of being hired. Any law firm experience, either summer clerkships or full-time, can be a plus on your résumé. It goes without saying that superior writing skills are demanded.

On the personal side, a pleasing personality, a high energy level, and a large supply of enthusiasm are necessary assets. Your people skills, communication, the ability to deal with a wide range of people, should be well honed. Being well organized will help you to sift through the sheer bulk of information and to perform the variety of tasks for which you will be responsible.

## JOB RESPONSIBILITIES ♦ ENTRY LEVEL

Most individual legislator's offices include persons with the titles and responsibilities described below. Some variations exist in titles and salaries, but the work that must be done is quite similar throughout Congress and at the state level.

Administrative assistants typically combine political work with legislative and managerial functions. Persons in this position may both run the office and serve as the legislator's confidante.

Legislative assistants or aides perform most of the research and writing related to drafting bills. They also assist their senator or representative on the floor or in committee hearings. Predictably, this group of assistants is a prime target of lobbyists. In addition, they handle legislative aspects of constituent questions and draft the technical portions of newsletters for the home state or district.

Constituent services specialists or caseworkers do exactly what their titles suggest: They keep the voters happy, and this may encompass anything from organizing tours of the Pentagon to helping a disgruntled Social Security recipient through the byzantine maze of the bureaucracy.

Support staff make up the backbone of every office and handle the paper flow. While this is not a position to which most budding lawyers aspire, it has been said that "Everyone on the Hill types except one or two senators," and what better way to learn?

Committee and subcommittee staffs offer more opportunities for lawyers, and are organized along the following lines.

Majority counsel/staff director reports to the chairman and ranking member of the committee. This individual is responsible for all legislative matters that fall within the committee's jurisdiction, but most particularly for those reflecting the ranking legislator's interests. He or she also is responsible for committee hiring. If the committee is large, these areas of responsibility may be divided between two people.

Minority counsel performs similar functions for the ranking representative of the political party that is not in control.

Assistant counsel and professional staff are persons with substantive expertise in the area of the committee's work. They do the bulk of the research, legislative drafting, and prepare committee reports and other written materials.

Chief clerk coordinates the committee's hearing schedule, and manages the office.

Support staff performs the same functions as in members' offices.

## MOVING UP

Unless a staff person feels special loyalty to a particular senator or representative, moving up on the Hill typically means moving to a committee. Not only do the committees pay a little more, but their staffs generally are insulated from the massive changes that occur on personal staffs after each election. In addition, an attorney doing committee work can very quickly become an expert in the areas that fall within that committee's jurisdiction. Member staffs, by contrast, must be generalists, with some information about a wide variety of subjects in order to serve constituents relying on a very small office as their key contact in Washington, DC.

More often than not, however, moving up means moving out, especially if you already are a member of a committee staff. Those who move out most often take positions lobbying, positions with law firms, or corporate and trade association positions. They may rely on expertise in active areas of practice, which they developed in the course of their committee assignments, or they may simply decide that they want to practice law and that now is the time to do so.

One to three years' legislative staff experience is quite a valuable credential for a young lawyer. However, staying on the Hill longer than that in a legislative staff position can make it difficult to find work commensurate with your expertise and salary expectations. Firms will be more reluctant to pay an older lawyer with five to six years' experience a training period salary (and you will find it harder to accept) than a staffer with only one or two years of experience. Placement directors recommend that you should have your eyes open during your entire legislative tenure, looking for the area in which you can most profitably use your skills and pursue long-term career goals.

## SALARIES

Only one safe generalization applies to salaries on the Hill—they are significantly lower than salaries in the Washington, DC, law firms: Hill salaries are within the discretion of individual members, and good jobs have been known to go for as little as $12,000 per year.

An individual who finds a good fit in job terms, however, can increase salary very quickly. The average salary of a House committee staff member, for example, is more than $40,000 per year.

## WORKING CONDITIONS

**HOURS:** Legislative work is characterized by long hours when the legislature is in session, and occasionally by 24-hour stints as a recess approaches.

**ENVIRONMENT:** Surroundings will be comfortable, but in no way lavish in government offices. Offices may be somewhat crowded, but this is becoming less the case as additional office space continues to be built in Washington, DC.

**WORKSTYLE:** In individual members' offices, staffers will find themselves doing a number of jobs simultaneously, and must be capable of switching from one subject area to another quickly. Committee staffers may be somewhat more focused, but still will have to respond to numerous telephone calls or requests for their time from congressional sponsors and lobbyists.

**TRAVEL:** Except to accompany a legislator on a fact-finding mission, travel is not generally part of the committee staffer's job. Personal staff travels entirely at the legislator's discretion.

## INTERNSHIPS

Summer internships are available in most members' offices, as well as in many committees and subcommittees. Experience obtained during an internship is extremely valuable for students of legislative and political processes. Also, because no intern can afford to assume that a permanent position will automatically be forthcoming in the office where he or she works as an intern, the summer can be spent learning one's way around and developing contacts that will help in the search for a full-time job.

Interns frequently will be assigned research and writing projects for which the regular staff may not have had time, but which nonetheless are very important to the success of the office. Every intern still should expect to do some scut work, especially if the internship is in a legislator's office. Constituent services inevitably are a major portion of the workload in these settings, and can become grueling for the permanent staff because of their range and quantity in relation to the size of that staff. An intern who wants to be remembered fondly as a member of the team is well advised to offer to carry some of that load.

Internships are almost the only Capitol Hill jobs for which there is an identifiable time period during which to make applications. Interested students should submit their résumés between late winter and early spring. Bulletins advertising openings are posted in your law school placement office, but students can get a jump on the process by writing to their home state representatives or senators before the official notices go out. The home state advantage in getting these internships cannot be emphasized enough. Those from less populous states located far from Washington, DC, have the advantage over students from states such as New York, Pennsylvania, or Maryland. Would-be interns should be aware that most positions are on a volunteer basis, and that the supply of interested applicants exceeds the number of available positions. Students who must earn money during the summer in order to return to school in the fall will want to explore alternate sources of funding through their financial aid offices.

## RECOMMENDED READING

**BOOKS**

*The Almanac of American Politics*, by Michael Barone and Grand Ujifusa, National Journal: revised biannually

*Congressional Staff Directory*, Congressional Quarterly, Inc.: revised annually

*Encyclopedia of Associations*, Gale Research Co.: revised biannually

*National Directory of Corporate Public Affairs*, Columbia Books: revised annually

*National Trade and Professional Association*, Columbia Books: revised annually

*Who Runs Congress?* by Mark Green with Michael Waldman, Dell Books: 1984

**ARTICLES**

"Power Politics: How the Nuclear Power Lobby Won Big on Capitol Hill," by V. Novak and S. Kaplan, *Common Cause Magazine*, January/February 1988.

"The Persuasive Powers of Corporate Lobbyists," by Ronald E. Kisner, *Black Enterprise*, April 1984.

"What Every Lobbyist Should Know," by J.L. Swerdlow, *Channels*, February 1987.

## PROFESSIONAL ASSOCIATIONS

American League of Lobbyists
1133 Fifteenth Street, N.W.
Washington, DC 20005

National Conference of State Legislators
1125 Seventeenth Street, Suite 1500
Denver, CO 80202

# INTERVIEWS

## MINORITY COUNSEL AND STAFF DIRECTOR
## U.S. SENATE COMMITTEE
## WASHINGTON, DC

Commitee counsels in the Senate assist senators and committees in everything from drafting legislation and writing reports to running hearings and answering legislative questions for senators' constituents and staff. Some function strictly as legal technicians. The Office of Legislative Counsel in the Senate is an example of these. It is filled with excellent lawyers who have decided to specialize in writing legislation. Someone in my capacity would write a memo describing needed legislation and what it should accomplish, and the lawyers in the office of legislative counsel draft the legislation according to those specifications. Most, however, have responsibilities in particular policy areas like tax, trade, civil rights and others.

The amount of freedom to develop legislative proposals that a committee lawyer has depends, to a great extent, upon the relationship that lawyer has with the senator who appointed him or her. If the senator trusts your judgment and likes your ideas, he or she will let you run with them and will provide support when it's needed. By and large, the lawyers who serve committees are very good lawyers; they write excellent reports and proposals, prepare good questions for hearings, and manage the hearings so that those questions are answered. The same kinds of things one would do in private practice. Some, though, are purely politicians.

The quality of experience a lawyer obtains on the Hill can vary widely. A person can get a job with a well-known senator, but that senator can turn out to be difficult to work for and the job will prove disappointing. Other people end up accepting positions with little-known senators, and the jobs turn out to be very rewarding. Much depends on circumstances and the chemistry between the lawyer and his or her senator.

This is a very competitive job area right now for recent graduates. People coming out of law schools are accustomed to direct, on-campus recruiting, and I don't think you'll ever find any Senator interviewing on-campus. In that sense, hiring on the hill is both idiosyncratic and a process of self-selection. Unfortunately, not everyone who looks for a job with Congress is successful.

Opportunities for legislative staffers do seem to be growing fairly rapidly at the state level. State governments are developing more sophistication and complexity, and they are beginning to have many more agencies and regulatory bodies. For persons who ultimately want to move to Congress, it certainly would be possible to transfer experience acquired in state government to Washington.

To get a legislative job, cynics might say it helps to be related to a major contributor—and I suppose it does. But a lot of people who try are able to find jobs with committees. The route I followed, writing letters from Chicago, is not the usual path to success, but it worked for me. Ordinarily, it helps to walk the halls and develop a network of contacts among people on the Hill who keep an eye out for openings and who will tell you when a position becomes available. Anyone who wants to work with Congress, though, should realize that turnover on the Hill is not what it used to be—it's lower, largely because the jobs are fun, there are few other opportunities for Democrats, and the Washington law market is somewhat glutted.

If there is a "typical" development pattern for lawyers doing legislative work, probably it is a function of their life-long interest in politics. My own path may be fairly characteristic. I did an undergraduate degree and major paper in government, and a Master's degree in political science. When I decided to go to law school, it was largely because I thought it would make me more effective politically. My choice of law schools, jobs and extracurricular activities was made with politics in the back of my mind.

If I were advising a student about undergraduate preparation, I would recommend going to a good college and obtaining a well-rounded education with background in political science, history, and economics. They could also benefit by improving their writing skills by working on college newspapers and, possibly, political campaigns. Active campaigning for someone, and that may include giving speeches or writing some of the candidate's speeches, develops many of the same skills one uses as a legislative staffer.

My advice to a law student would be similar: a good law school; a good general legal education, with a focus on developing writing skills; and some political activities outside the law school. It is a lot of work, but law students benefit from having enough experience with politics and government to decide whether they really want to be legislative staffers. There are all kinds of internships and other programs with legislative bodies.

Law students considering legislative work are often concerned about limiting their long-range career options. They need to realize that many of their functions as committee counsels are comparable to what they would do in private practice—the analogy to negotiating contracts is a good example. In order to negotiate the language of a piece of legislation, you must not only be able to do the drafting; you must also have done the research necessary to know the background of the problem and enable you to argue your position.

In other words, the legal skills are transferable if you decide you want to go somewhere else with them. It is, however, undeniably true that staying "too long" in the government can pose lateral entry problems unless one develops a marketable specialty. This concern should not be paralyzing, but it should be recognized.

The personal skills and qualities required for success in legislative work primarily relate to getting along with people. It's not enough to be a good attorney and know your area. Committee lawyers and legislators' staffers have to be able to relate well to their co-workers and the public. A lawyer may win in court by grinding his opponent into chalkdust in front of a judge, but a person who is perceived as being unpleasantly aggressive won't do well on the Hill. Here, you have to be able to convince people to support your position, to build coalitions, and to work repeatedly with people. If you have treated someone badly—for example, not done something you promised to do—it will come back to haunt you. If you cannot agree with someone's position, it is better just to tell them that and not be devious.

For me, the most rewarding aspect of this kind of work is that it's naturally challenging: coming up with new ideas to implement a senator's goals, translating these ideas into written documents and legislation, and building the political support necessary to implement them is a complex and very demanding process. I also like the fact that the work is extremely varied, no two days are the same. The third, and perhaps the most rewarding aspect of legislative work, is that you work on public sector issues that almost always are important and that have a tremendous impact on people's lives.

Probably the most disappointing aspect of the job for me is circumstantial—it's being in the minority! That can happen regardless of one's abilities, and it's frustrating because it does limit what you can accomplish.

During the typical week, my time is fairly evenly divided among in-office paperwork; meetings with colleagues to exchange information and ideas, or negotiations; meetings with the senator; and telephone work with the press, the public, or other people on the Hill. I find I have to be careful not to lose my perspective about time. Your work isn't done once you have written the bill. You can go on to write newspaper articles in support of the bill, write speeches for the same purpose, spend hours monitoring support and meeting with lobbyists or others on the Hill to increase support—the list goes on and on. There is so much to do that sometimes you feel like you're pushing a boulder up a large hill with your nose! I have a family with two small children, and it's very important for me to be able to spend time with them and my wife.

The time commitment required to be productive in this kind of position is at least 9 AM to 6:30 PM every day in the office, with about ten hours of work at home each week in the evenings. But generally I have not had to work weekends, and I have not had to travel much. I have many friends in private practice who never see their families at all, so I am pleased with the balance I have been able to obtain.

While this kind of life is not particularly hard by the standards of some people, like merger and acquisition lawyers, it's not particularly easy either. You have tremendous responsibility for issues that can affect thousands of people. Consequently you don't cut corners. But I have been very happy in this job, and although other options sometimes beckon, it will take an unusual combination of circumstances for me to find another job so challenging and rewarding.

CAROLYN JOURDAN
ASSOCIATE COUNSEL
U.S. SENATE COMMITTEE ON ENVIRONMENT AND
PUBLIC WORKS
WASHINGTON, DC

For me, the decision to pursue a career in law was a random choice that worked out. My first career choice was engineering. In fact, I earned a degree in biomedical engineering from the University of Tennessee. I was all set to pursue a career as an engineer, but then I learned a very tough, and disturbing, lesson: Companies just weren't interested in hiring female engineers.

It was at this point that I made my decision to go to law school, also at the University of Tennessee. After I graduated, I tried landing a job in Tennessee but had no luck. Fortunately, though, I got a big break, when I was offered a clerkship with the Federal District Court in Miami. After my two-year clerkship, doors finally started opening for me.

I started working for the Senate about two-and-a-half years ago for Senator Jim Sasser, Democrat of Tennessee, as Chief Counsel to his Subcommittee on the Committee on Governmental Affairs. A few months ago I switched to the Committee on Environment and

Public Works. Chairman Quentin Burdick, Democrat of North Dakota, employs me to assist Senator John Breaux, Democrat of Louisiana, on the Subcommittee on Nuclear Regulation which he chairs.

Committee work is very cyclical. There is a big, two-year cycle and a smaller monthly cycle that operate at the same time. A "congress" lasts for two years, and the Senate is not in session for about one week per month. When the Senate is in session I work on hearings and debates and votes on the Senate floor. When the Senate is not in session I work on drafting and negotiating legislation, oversight of agencies, investigations, answering mail, and meeting with people who have an interest in nuclear power.

In some ways, the quality of your job as a committee staffer depends on the Senator to whom you are assigned. In this respect, I have found working with Sen. Breaux to be particularly rewarding. In addition to being a long-time Congressman, Sen. Breaux himself served as a staffer. He encourages his staff members to take an active approach toward their work, and he keeps in close contact with us. This helps make my job very pleasant and rewarding.

## JULIE ANN SPIEZIO
### COUNSEL
### AMERICAN COUNCIL OF LIFE INSURANCE, WASHINGTON, DC

I started working for the American Council of Life Insurance about four years ago, as a Legislative Associate and Attorney. I held that position for about two years, when I assumed my current role of Legislative Director and Counsel.

A number of factors conspired to bring me to where I am today. I first became interested in government relations when I was a student at Marquette University in Milwaukee, WI. At Marquette, I became involved in the student government program. As part of the program, I was given the opportunity to lobby with the U.S.

Students Association for student issues. I went to Washington and met with Congressional representatives from our home state of Wisconsin.

After graduating from law school in Saint Louis, I moved to Washington, DC. I interviewed for several positions in various government agencies, private firms, and trade associations. After much thought and consideration, I made what I consider to be a quality-of-life decision, and chose to work for a large, private industry trade group.

I have found that working for a trade association like the American Council of Life Insurance is a happy medium between the high pressure of private firms and the near-tedium of some other aspects of the law. Attorneys for trade associations don't make as much money as lawyers at private firms do, but compensation and benefits are well above what is available in a career in government. In addition, as a government relations specialist for a trade association, I get more hands-on experience in government relations than I would get actually working for the government.

As counsel to my organization, I represent the life insurance industry on a wide range of issues, including health insurance and health care issues, banking, and investments. Although I am based in Washington, a great deal of the lobbying I do is performed in the various states where I have the primary responsibility of representing the industry's positions. Lobbying for the insurance industry is a little different because the industry is regulated primarily by state governments.

I'm responsible for representing my organization's interests in five states: Indiana, Kansas, Oklahoma, Nebraska, and Alaska. During the legislative sessions in those states, I do a lot of first-person lobbying in the state houses. Those sessions generally last from the third week of January to sometime in August. Although I can plan my visiting schedules somewhat, the nature of the legislative process is that it is full of surprises. You get to know what to expect, and you come to expect the unexpected.

# PRIVATE PRACTICE

The private practice of law offers an exceedingly wide range of career opportunities. No other profession encompasses a greater variety of work experiences than may be found in our country's 175,000-plus legal establishments—a term that includes small general practice firms, large multioffice firms, and every type and size in between. Such diversity defies generalization, except in the broadest sense; however, private law practice as a whole is clearly a booming business, with gross revenues growing at double-digit rates annually.

Significant among the reasons for this rapid growth rate are the removal of restrictions on lawyer advertising, increased numbers of legal clinics and prepaid legal services plans that provide legal services to middle-income groups, and the growing complexity of the economy. These factors have also promoted increased public awareness of individual and collective rights, which in turn provides more work for more lawyers.

Finding the perfect job is not as easy as it may sound, however, for the more than 35,000 students who graduate each year from the 175 American Bar Association-accredited law schools in the United States. A recent survey of graduating law students by the National Association of Law Placement revealed that about 62 percent of these graduates enter private practice, with about a quarter of them being hired by very large (100+ attorneys) firms that serve as counsel to the major corporations and financial institutions that comprise U.S. big business. To many of you, this statistic may seem surprisingly small, since these megafirms are the most publicly visible. Theirs is the world of corporate mergers and acquisitions, takeover battles, major real estate transactions, and complex securities offerings. Theirs is also the world of on-campus recruiting, and they uniformly place great emphasis on academic credentials. Top students at nationally acclaimed law schools may find that they need look no further than their school's placement office to find employment with a very large firm, but most students at most schools will find this option unavailable to them.

The fact is, however, that the proportion of law school graduates landing jobs with very large firms is increasing rapidly. In the early 1980s, less than 10 percent of the graduating class was finding work at very large firms. The National Association of Law Placement projects that by the turn of the century, the institutional lawyer—that is, the lawyer who works for a megafirm—is likely to be the predominant form of practitioner in the legal profession.

Less than half of the new hires in private practice work for law firms with 25 or fewer attorneys. These small firms provide legal services to many of the country's small businesses, as well as specialized services for many larger companies. In addition, they handle legal problems for individual clients, including real estate transactions, divorces and other domestic relations issues, estate planning and drafting of wills, personal injury actions, and defense against criminal charges. Very few law firms attempt to handle all of these types of work, and many specialize by area of practice, such as criminal defense or tax litigation, or by whom they represent, for example, plaintiffs' personal injury or defendant's medical malpractice.

Medium-sized firms (25–100 attorneys) employ the remaining 30 percent or so of new hires in private practice. Most of these firms have characteristics of both their larger and smaller counterparts, though some, particularly those composed of lawyers who have split off from a very large firm or firms, are virtually indistinguishable from large firms in terms of workstyle and hiring criteria.

## JOB OUTLOOK

**JOB OPENINGS WILL GROW:** About as fast as average

**COMPETITION FOR JOBS:** Keen

Competition is keen for entry-level positions with all large law firms and with smaller law firms offering good salaries in most parts of the country. The situation is particularly acute in areas that are inundated with lawyers, such as California and New York, NY.

**NEW JOB OPPORTUNITIES:** Demand for legal services rises and falls with national and local shifts in politics, and the hot areas in law practice today are mergers and acquisitions, bankruptcy, real estate, and tax, while decreased governmental regulation has lessened the demand for lawyers in such areas as labor law, environmental law, and antitrust law. Rapid-fire technological advances in areas ranging from telecommunications to new life forms have opened up a new world of job opportunities for lawyers with backgrounds in science and engineering.

Also look for increased job opportunities in areas involving alternatives to litigation as a means of resolving disputes. Current trends include neighborhood justice centers and divorce mediation. The growth in prepaid legal care plans will require increased numbers of specialists to deal with new problems involving such areas as Social Security and worker's compensation.

## GEOGRAPHIC JOB INDEX

Not surprisingly, the largest law firms are located primarily in the nation's largest cities. New York is home to 32 of the nation's 100 largest law firms, followed by Chicago, San Francisco, Los Angeles, Philadelphia, Cleveland, Boston, Houston, and Washington. Other cities that are home to some of the country's biggest law firms include Atlanta, Baltimore, Columbus, OH, Dallas, Denver, Detroit, Minneapolis, Omaha, Pittsburgh, Richmond, VA, Rochester,

NY, Saint Louis, and Seattle. Just about all of the top 100 law firms have branch offices in several cities, and eight of the top 20 have offices abroad to serve the expanding needs of their large national and multinational corporate clients.

Small firms are located in virtually every big city and small town in the country, though the types of law practiced may vary considerably in urban versus rural areas. You should bear in mind, however, that many small firms strongly prefer to hire new associates from local law schools because they believe, rightly or wrongly, that local students will be a better "fit" with the other lawyers in the firm in terms of personality, background, and life-style. Consequently, unless you plan to attend one of a handful of nationally known schools, your future geographic preference should be a factor in your decision regarding which law school to attend.

## WHO THE EMPLOYERS ARE

**LARGE MULTI-OFFICE FIRMS** represent very large corporate clients, national or international in scope. Virtually all of the 100 largest and many of the 200 largest firms in the country fit this definition.

**MEDIUM-SIZED FIRMS** vary in size, though they usually are not as large as the principal offices of multioffice firms in the same region. They represent locally or regionally prominent clients, and may have branch offices in the state, in the region, or in Washington, DC.

**SMALL FIRMS** may be general practices, handling a wide variety of legal matters for individuals and small businesses, or specialists in one or a few areas of practice.

**LEGAL CLINICS AND OTHER PRIVATE LEGAL SERVICES** provide a wide range of routine legal services to the public for lower cost than is charged by most other law firms.

## MAJOR LAW FIRMS

| CITY AND FIRM | TOTAL NUMBER OF LAWYERS |
|---|---|
| **ATLANTA** | |
| King & Spalding | 214 |
| Powell, Goldstein, Frazer & Murphy | 183 |
| Alston & Bird | 172 |
| **BOSTON** | |
| Ropes & Gray | 262 |
| Hale & Dorr | 253 |
| Goodwin, Procter & Hoar | 225 |
| **CHICAGO** | |
| Baker & McKenzie | 1040 |
| Sidley & Austin | 570 |
| Mayer, Brown & Platt | 414 |
| **CLEVELAND** | |
| Jones, Day, Reavis & Pogue | 817 |
| Baker & Hostetler | 382 |
| Squire, Sanders & Dempsey | 340 |
| **DALLAS** | |
| Akin, Gump, Strauss, Hauer & Feld | 343 |
| Johnson & Swanson, P.C. | 198 |
| Thompson & Knight | 183 |
| **HOUSTON** | |
| Fulbright & Jaworski | 434 |
| Vinson & Elkins | 413 |
| Baker & Botts | 330 |

**LOS ANGELES**

| | |
|---|---|
| Gibson, Dunn & Crutcher | 596 |
| Latham & Watkins | 434 |
| O'Melveny & Myers | 411 |

**NEW YORK**

| | |
|---|---|
| Skadden, Arps, Slate, Meagher & Flom | 828 |
| Sherarman & Sterling | 504 |
| Weil, Gotshal & Manges | 445 |

**PHILADELPHIA**

| | |
|---|---|
| Morgan, Lewis & Bockius | 604 |
| Pepper, Hamilton & Scheetz | 306 |
| Dechert Price & Rhoads | 300 |

**SAN FRANCISCO**

| | |
|---|---|
| Pillsbury, Madison & Sutro | 478 |
| Morrison & Foerster | 373 |
| Brobeck, Phleger & Harrison | 328 |

**WASHINGTON**

| | |
|---|---|
| Arnold & Porter | 279 |
| Hogan & Hartson | 252 |
| Covington & Burling | 234 |

Source: The *Of Counsel 500* of 1988

## HOW TO BREAK INTO THE FIELD

There is only one sure formula for getting a job with a large corporate law firm: good grades at a prestigious law school. Large firms typically fill their openings through on-campus interviews, and they strongly prefer to hire students from those schools at which they recruit. If your school does not have a large on-campus recruiting program, a letter-writing campaign to large firms in your geographic area may net you some interviews, but only if you have superb grades or law review experience. Timing is critical, too; large firms do virtually all of their hiring during the August to November recruiting season. It is also important to begin this process during the fall of your second year of law school, because many firms fill most of their permanent openings by making offers to students who have worked for them as summer associates following their second year of law school.

Unlike large firms, which have predictable and recurring hiring needs, small firms usually hire new lawyers only occasionally, and then only when their needs are immediate. Consequently, these firms adhere to no established timetables. Getting hired is often a matter of making the right contacts and being in the right place at the right time. The hiring criteria are different, too. Many of these firms view academic performance as much less important than personality and street smarts.

A law student who seeks a position with a small firm should bear in mind the following:

1. Unless you have spectacular credentials, a few well-focused inquiries addressed to specific individuals at firms in which you have a genuine interest will carry you much farther than a mass mailing of form letters.

2. If you don't know many lawyers in the geographic area in which you wish to practice, add job search preparation to your agenda as soon as you enter law school. Get in touch with lawyers who are alumni of your law school or undergraduate institution. Talk to your professors and fellow students. Read the local law journal so that you can become aware of which lawyers are prominent in which substantive areas of the law. All of this will be valuable to you later on. In addition, the American Bar Association and most state and local bar associations have law student divisions that can be important sources of information about various types of law practice.

3. Be certain that your résumé and cover letter are perfect examples of your best work; they must be neat, concise, and error-free. Emphasize in your letter what you can do for the firm—not what it can do for you.

4. Remember that many small firms don't hire law school graduates until they have passed the bar exams. Timing is critical. The same letter written to the same person at the same firm at two different times may yield vastly different results.

There are several excellent sources of information about large and medium-sized law firms, including the two-volume *American Lawyer Guide to Leading Law Firms* and the firms' "résumés" and National Association for Law Placement data forms that nearly every law school placement office makes available to its students. The only general reference guide to firms of all sizes is the seven-volume *Martindale-Hubbell Law Directory*, which provides biographical information and areas of specialization for most law firms.

## INTERNATIONAL JOB OPPORTUNITIES

Only 44 of the 250 largest law firms in the United States have branch offices in foreign countries, but many other large firms advise their clients with respect to international business, banking, and tax matters. The chances for an overseas assignment, even for experienced, high-level lawyers, are slim, but there is opportunity for travel abroad at firms with international business. Very little public sector international law (the kind taught in most international law courses in law school) is practiced by private law firms, and most small firms do not deal with international matters at all.

## LARGE FIRMS

Most large firms are divided into departments along practice lines, for example, corporate, litigation, real estate, tax, trust and estates.

New associates are usually assigned to one department immediately, but may be given the opportunity in some firms to try out work from a variety of departments before their "marriage" to a particular area of practice. This is a critical decision, because it determines an attorney's future job opportunities. It is very difficult to find employment as a corporate lawyer, for example, if one has been working as a litigator previously.

At all firms the partners are the owners, and the associates are employees, but most large firms have a much more rigid hierarchical structure than do small ones. An associate who aspires to partnership at a large firm must pass through a 5–10 year trial period, at the end of which time he or she is either made a partner or expected to find other employment. With the exception of a very few law firms that have recently established a class of permanent specialists in such areas as pensions or state securities laws, there is no middle ground, the name of the game is up or out. The odds against being made partner are great indeed; fewer than one in ten entry-level associates at most large firms will ever move into the ownership ranks. Of course, many associates don't stick around for the day of reckoning. Some are asked to leave early on, while others voluntarily move to corporations, financial institutions, and smaller firms, where they find that their large-firm credentials are well-respected.

## QUALIFICATIONS

**PERSONAL:** Objectivity. A high regard for precision and detail. Ability to be a team player. Physical and mental stamina.

**PROFESSIONAL:** Excellent legal research and writing skills. Finely honed analytical skills.

## CAREER PATHS

| LEVEL | JOB TITLE | EXPERIENCE NEEDED |
|---|---|---|
| Entry | Associate | Law degree |
| 2 | Partner | 5–10 years |
| (2) | (Permanent associate) | (Varies; only an option in specialized areas of a few large firms) |

## JOB RESPONSIBILITIES ◆ ENTRY LEVEL

**THE BASICS:** Entry-level associates may rotate through departments in the firm, or they may be assigned to one area of practice from the beginning. In either event, during their first few years of practice most associates spend the majority of their time working on narrow aspects of large cases or projects.

**MORE CHALLENGING DUTIES:** Some degree of client contact; responsibility for small cases and projects in their entirety and more complex aspects of large cases or projects; less-structured assignments.

## MOVING UP

There is no magic pathway to partnership in a large firm. However, hard work, the ability to get along well with clients and to bring in new ones, and the firm's needs in the associate's area of expertise all are key components. Firm politics also plays a role, so it is almost impossible for any senior associate to predict with certainty that he or she will ultimately be made a partner. As a result, the pressure mounts after associates complete their first few years of practice, and many are lured away from large firms by jobs that require a less intensive time commitment or offer more predictable long-term career stability. Those who remain work harder than ever in an effort to enhance their chances of winning the partnership sweepstakes.

Upward mobility does not cease once an associate becomes a partner, although there are no subsequent title designations that proclaim to the outside world that one partner is more prominent than another. Generally those partners who are responsible for the firm's key clients and the most lucrative areas of the firm's practice have the strongest voice in firm management issues and receive the largest shares of the firm's profits. A partner who finds that his or her area of expertise is more valuable elsewhere may move to another firm, and prominent partners are often sought after for high government posts, corporate chief executive slots, and prestigious teaching positions.

## SMALL FIRMS

Small firms are the backbone of our country's legal system. Structurally, they run the gamut from miniature versions of large firms to essentially nonhierarchical entities in which everyone is a partner. The former are primarily found in the larger cities, while small-town law practices generally have fewer than ten attorneys and are more loosely knit.

Lawyers in small firms may have more personal freedom than do those in larger firms, and they usually have the opportunity to work closely with clients at a relatively early stage in their legal careers. They generally have responsibility for all aspects of a case or project and are less likely to feel that they are working on trees in somebody else's forest. Long-term job stability is more common at a small firm than at a larger one, but a small firm has few major steady clients, and so may be at a greater risk as an ongoing entity than a larger firm.

### QUALIFICATIONS

**PERSONAL:** Good organizational abilities. Empathy. Ability to think on your feet and speak extemporaneously.

**PROFESSIONAL:** Legal research and writing skills. Client counseling and negotiation skills.

### CAREER PATHS

| LEVEL | JOB TITLE | EXPERIENCE NEEDED |
|-------|-----------|-------------------|
| Entry | Associate or partner | Law degree |
| 2 | Partner | 3–10+ years (although this varies widely depending on the firm) |

## JOB RESPONSIBILITIES ◆ ENTRY LEVEL

**THE BASICS:** Heavy emphasis on research and writing, but many have client contact from the beginning.

**MORE CHALLENGING DUTIES:** Involvement in all phases of the litigation process, including taking depositions and making appearances in court.

## MOVING UP

Opportunities for upward mobility in small firms vary considerably, so it is important for the beginning associate to assess the firm structurally and historically to determine what his or her long-range prospects there may be. Some small firms, for example, have a fixed partnership structure and employ a continually changing pool of associates who have no real hope of advancement. Others—particularly those with a high percentage of institutional rather than individual clients—function more like the larger firms and have similar "up or out" policies. Nearly all small firms, however, place great emphasis on a person's "rainmaking ability"—potential for drawing new business to the firm. In many, a substantial client base is a prerequisite to partnership.

# ADDITIONAL INFORMATION

According to a recent survey by the National Association of Law Placement, starting salaries at the nation's largest law firms averaged about $48,000 per year. The average was highest in New York, where according to the publication *Of Counsel*, starting salaries in Manhattan law firms had reached $70,000. In contrast, the big law firms in Philadelphia—just 100 miles away from New York—paid average starting salaries of about $50,000. In New York, associates with five years' experience typically earned more than $80,000 in that year.

At the partner level, compensation varies widely both between firms and within them. Almost all partners make at least twice as much money as the most senior associates at their respective firms, however, and partners at some of the largest firms each take home several hundreds of thousands of dollars annually.

Smaller firms generally pay considerably lower starting salaries than do larger firms. There are a number of reasons for this differential, but the major one is that they usually bill their clients less per hour for their services than do larger firms. Many small firms are more entrepreneurial in their approach to compensation and will reward associates who bring in new clients with a share in the fees generated from the business. Some small firms—particularly those that do a great deal of work on a contingency basis—pay bonuses in good years. Although most large firm partners make more money than partners in small firms, some of the wealthiest lawyers in the country are solo or small firm superstars. In general, however, law is not a highly lucrative profession, and those whose primary expectations are monetary will probably be disappointed.

## WORKING CONDITIONS

### LARGE FIRMS

**HOURS:** Most large firms have support staff working in shifts around the clock, and on occasion (e.g., during a contested takeover battle or a complicated financing) you will almost certainly be expected to work all night. The increase in starting salaries over the past few years certainly have come with strings attached. In those high-paying New York law firms, for instance, associates are sometimes expected to produce 55 to 60 billable hours of work *per week*—a feat that usually can only be accomplished by working six or seven days a week. The expected production at smaller firms may not be as daunting, but few attorneys at private firms work only 40-hour weeks.

**ENVIRONMENT:** Lawyers in large firms usually work in luxuriously appointed suites of offices, complete with the latest in telephone and computer-assisted research technology. Junior associates may be expected to share an office and a secretary with another associate for a year or two, but few lawyers in large firms will find their workspaces cramped or uncomfortable. And large-firm lawyers are expected to dress in a manner befitting their surroundings; the "uniform" for both men and women is a conservative suit with an equally conservative shirt or blouse.

**WORKSTYLE:** A new law school graduate knows very little about the realities of law practice, so large firms typically spend a great deal of time and effort in one form or another of associate training. Some firms have formal continuing legal education programs, while others take a team or one-to-one mentor approach to the development of lawyering skills. In nearly every large firm, however, junior litigation associates spend a great deal of time researching and writing legal memorandums or working on pretrial discovery matters, and junior corporate, real estate, and tax associates work on basic projects and the more routine aspects of complex transactions. Those lawyers who demonstrate that they have acquired sophisticated legal skills are gradually given more responsibility and are most likely to be selected to work on the most interesting (and time-consuming) cases or projects.

**TRAVEL:** As a junior associate you are likely to travel very little—if at all—and then only if the senior associates or partners need someone to tend to administrative tasks. Senior associates may travel to corporate closings or to do discovery or take depositions in connection with complex litigation. The latter, in particular, can require extended periods of time away from home. Foreign travel opportunities may arise if the firm has a multinational clientele, but truly desirable trips are usually reserved for partners.

**SMALL FIRMS**
**HOURS:** The private practice of law offers few nine-to-five jobs, and opportunities with small firms are no exception to this rule; clients

of any size firm must be diligently served when their legal needs arise if the practice is to thrive. Some smaller firms do, however, allow greater flexibility in exchange for a smaller paycheck, and may even permit associates to do other legal work on the side if they are entrepreneurially inclined. This is not by any means always the case, however, and it is much more common in firms that represent individuals on a single-case basis (e.g., a personal injury case or preparation of a will) than in firms that represent businesses or wealthy individuals on an ongoing basis.

**ENVIRONMENT:** "Have legal pad, will travel" is an apt motto for junior associates at many smaller firms. Your "office" may be the corner of a conference room or a tiny cubicle next to a secretary or another lawyer—or it may be as elegant as the office of an associate at the largest firm in town. More and more smaller firms have started to share space with each other to minimize overhead costs and to finance jointly such costly necessities as libraries, computer services, and photocopying facilities.

**WORKSTYLE:** As a junior associate much of your time will most likely be spent either in the library or en route to court to make routine appearances. Your life will probably be less structured than that of your counterpart in a large firm, and you will be more likely to work in most or all of the substantive areas of your firm's practice.

**TRAVEL:** Unless you include trips to and from the courthouse in your definition of "travel," you probably won't travel much during your career as a lawyer in a small firm.

## INTERNSHIPS

Virtually every large law firm has a formal summer associate program for law students who have completed two years of study. Third-year students who aspire to large-firm practice may find offers of permanent employment difficult to obtain if they have not clerked for a large firm the previous summer. Summer associates do the same type of research and document preparation that first-year full-time associates do, but the real purpose of these programs is to give students and firms an opportunity to get to know each other. There are fringe benefits, too. Large firms go to great lengths—with top salaries, lavish dinners, parties, and nights on the town—to win the favor of the best students for whom they are all vying.

Very few small firms have established formal summer clerkship programs for law students, but many of them do hire students to work part-time during the school year and part-time or full-time during the summer. This type of apprenticeship has long been the traditional means bywhich most new attorneys have gained experience and found employment. You should be wary, however, of firms that exploit students by using them as little more than low-paid clerical workers. Unless a job offers solid legal training or a strong possibility of eventual full-time employment, it is probably not worth the time spent away from your studies.

Law firms of all sizes look favorably on students who have clerked for a judge during law school or after graduation. Judicial clerkships can be obtained at the municipal, state, or federal level, and students with prestigious federal circuit court or Supreme Court clerkship experience can almost write their own ticket to any large firm in the country.

## RECOMMENDED READING

### BOOKS

*American Lawyer Guide to Leading Law Firms*, compiled by the staff of *The American Lawyer*: revised periodically

*Law & Legal Information Directory*, Gale Research Co.: revised biannually

*Lawyering: A Realistic Approach to Legal Practice*, by James C. Freund, Doubleday & Company: 1982

*The Lawyers,* by Martin Meyer, Greenwood Press: 1980

*Lions of the Eighties: The Inside Story of the Powerhouse Law Firms,* by Paul Hoffman, Doubleday & Company: 1982

*Martindale-Hubbell Law Directory,* Martindale-Hubbel, Inc.: annual

*Parker Directory of Attorneys,* Parker & Son: revised annually

*Who's Who in American Law,* Marquis Who's Who: revised biannually

## PROFESSIONAL ASSOCIATION

American Bar Association
1155 East 60th Street
Chicago, IL 60637

# INTERVIEWS

### THIRD-YEAR ASSOCIATE
### MAJOR PRIVATE FIRM
### SAN FRANCISCO, CA

I wanted to go to law school because I was interested in politics and I thought it might be fun. Before I graduated I had decided I wanted to litigate, which to me meant being a trial lawyer. I looked at the kinds of firms that seemed to offer the fastest opportunity for a young lawyer to get in there and do it, as opposed to carrying someone's bags as they went and did it. This office is geared toward giving younger associates responsibility quickly because of the kind of work we're doing—insurance defense. There are more cases and the issues aren't as complex as in, say, antitrust work, so you're not just sitting in rooms sifting through documents.

The most enjoyable part of this job is when I go to court on something substantive, and I feel that I'm in control. The part of the job that isn't so exciting is going through files and doing paperwork. There's a lot more of that than I imagined.

The biggest shock to me has been seeing how often cases are settled out of court. I used to think that if your position was right you went in and fought it out. But your client might spend more money in paying for your defense of him than he would lose if he were to lose the trial. As a lawyer you have the duty to advise your client as to what is at risk and what it's going to cost to defend him, then, if there is a realistic settlement amount, you've got to be willing to advise him that it might be in his best interests to take it. These issues are usually business judgment questions. The myth for a young lawyer is that they will give you the small cases to handle on your own because there's not much at risk, and you'll get trial experience that way. More and more it is not economical to take even those small cases to trial. The long and short of being a young lawyer in a large private firm is that as a litigator you're a long way from being a trial lawyer.

## FOUNDING PARTNER
## WEST COAST LAW PRACTICE

I started the "adventure" as the youngest lawyer in a San Francisco admiralty firm. At that time I knew absolutely nothing about admiralty law—because I had gone to school in Chicago, where there was no great emphasis on admiralty law. But the interesting thing about law is that you don't have to know the specialty in order to become a reasonably good lawyer, because you learn on the job; it's one of the last existing apprenticeship professions.

From the admiralty firm I went to another firm where I began to learn something about litigation, which is, I think, more art than law. I stayed with that firm for three years, generally working for one of the older partners. It was he who decided—30 years ago—to start our firm, and he apparently needed someone to carry his briefcase. I started in that capacity, but when there were only two of us, it was very easy for me quickly to become a "name" partner. We thought we would have a kind of small-town friendly litigation practice, but we are now a large-city litigating firm because the large city grew around us.

Our firm is involved in all kinds of litigation, except for criminal work. I have principally tried cases in the fields of product liability, malpractice defense, and other civil areas, including actions for libel and slander. About nine out of ten civil cases are now disposed of without trial, though. You see, we have now reached the point where the underlying assumption of many judges is that litigants don't really have to use the court at all because they really should settle everything.

I think that potential lawyers should examine themselves carefully to be sure that they really want to be lawyers rather than that they like the *idea* of being lawyers, because the reality is quite different from the image. You put in a lot of hours and you work hard, and you should not be misled into thinking that it's always a joyful, wonderful, exhilarating experience. It is all this, in part, but since the trial is just the tip of the iceberg, and for every day in court you probably spend ten days in preparation, you can see that a lot of the work is drudgery. And it's an even worse situation now, since most cases are now settled. The satisfaction in litigation is not so much in winning as it is in doing well in light of your own standards. You may have lost the case, but if you know that you lost it for a lot less than anyone else would have lost it, you can be satisfied. Very often you know that because of your intervention a more just result occurred. We all recall our great wins, but other things also give us a feeling of satisfaction.

**JACK HUNDERMARK**
**ASSOCIATE**
**DIETRICH & ST. JOHN**
**TRENTON, NJ**

I graduated from law school in 1981 and walked right into a seller's market. There just weren't too many jobs available for law school graduates in the Philadelphia/Trenton area. Part of the reason was unfortunate timing. The early 1980s was the time of a tremendous glut of new lawyers. Unless you come from one of the nation's top law schools, or unless you graduate at the top of your class, that first job offer can be hard to come by.

It wasn't until late in 1981 that I got an offer from Dietrich & St. John. I joined the firm in December of that year. The first thing that surprised me about working in a private firm is the fact that you're left pretty much on your own to do your work. I expected more interaction with the senior members of the firm, but that wasn't the case.

I handle the bulk of the firm's litigation files. Most of the cases that I work on are personal-injury suits. I also do some mortgage foreclosures and collection cases. The first couple of years at the firm, I was also assigned a lot of divorce cases. One of the benefits of being at a firm for a few years is that you can pass some cases up. Divorce cases are detested by just about everyone. I now only handle uncontested divorce cases.

I do most of my work in the office—doing legal research, working on the telephone, drafting pleadings and the like. At Dietrich & St. John, we don't have a minimum quota of billable hours to meet, so the pace is not as hectic as it is at some other private firms, but there's enough work to keep us busy. In the course of a typical day, I'll work on about 12 to 15 different files.

Another aspect of private practice that has surprised me is the amount of time that you *don't* spend in court. In law school, students spend a lot of time preparing for trial work. Most cases are settled before they get to trial. On average, I make a courtroom appearance once every 10 days.

## SECOND-YEAR ASSOCIATE
## PRIVATE LAW FIRM

I am a second-year associate with a large firm best known for its representation of clients with multinational business interests.

Eighty percent of our clients are foreign clients, generally financial institutions and non-U.S. corporations, who have come to the United States to establish a branch or agency or to represent an existing office in its business transactions. My own personal experience within the firm may be somewhat atypical since I have been splitting my time between the litigation and the corporate/commercial departments in order to get a well-rounded look at the legal process.

In its hiring efforts, the firm tends to look for people who have some sort of international background. Most of my colleagues here have either lived abroad, are citizens of foreign countries, or are fluent in other languages. As for myself, I think the fact that I had worked on the *International and Comparative Law Review* in law school and had gone over to Europe for a summer to work in an English solicitors' firm helped me to obtain an offer from the firm. In addition, I am familiar with German and French, though I am not fluent.

From the outset of my legal education, I was extremely interested in the area of international law. During my last year of law school, I found out through interviews and research that generally the closest anyone can come to practicing true international law would be by working for the State Department or similar government agencies where you deal with treaties and the relations between countries. While a civil private practice in international business does often involve treaties and the like, our practice principally focuses upon international business transactions. I am often involved in drafting contracts, reviewing documentation, and giving advice on California and federal law as it applies to our client's situation. At times, we also look into another country's laws, but we will almost always advise the client to confirm those findings with a lawyer licensed in that particular country.

As a new lawyer in a firm there is a great deal of pressure to create a favorable reputation for yourself. In addition, you must learn to deal with a variety of personalities—a definite challenge within itself. The long hours that must often be put in make it difficult to have a social life simply because you become so exhausted that it is all you can do to get through the week, and then there is always the last-minute "I want you to do this" as you are walking out the door to have dinner with someone. Nevertheless, the hard work definitely does have its rewards, and after you have put forth your all, you do feel accomplished in knowing that you have learned new skills and have obtained a desirable result for your client.

## SENIOR PARTNER
## MAJOR PRIVATE FIRM
## LOS ANGELES, CA

The antitrust laws are designed to enforce a basic principle to which our society has dedicated itself: free and vigorous competition in the business sector. Antitrust lawyers who practice with the government enforce those laws to ensure that the open free market controls the process and development of products without collusion. Those of us in the private sector can be on both sides of that question. We can be defending companies and individuals who are charged with violating antitrust laws, or we can act almost as a private attorney general in a quasi-governmental function by bringing a private action on behalf of a company or individual who has been aggrieved by reason of an alleged violation of the antitrust laws.

One of the reasons I find antitrust law very interesting is that you're a litigator—a hired gun—but you are also involved in matters that affect national economy policy. It's intellectually stimulating and you can move from one industry to another in the course of your career. So it's not a narrow type of practice.

I would urge someone who wants to become an antitrust lawyer to study economics. That would be invaluable, as you'll work with consulting economists on a regular basis. What is most important, though, is analytical ability—to deal with legal questions, to analyze them, to see ahead in terms of the consequences of taking this step or that step. It's an intellectual profession, and the intellectually curious will find it very satisfying.

## SENIOR PARTNER
## PRIVATE LAW FIRM
## LOS ANGELES, CA

I am head of the labor department of a very large law firm that handles all types of legal problems for businesses. In the labor area we represent management—employers—in three broad categories of cases: traditional labor law, which involves employers and unions; employment discrimination law; and wrongful discharge litigation. Two of these three areas are new since I've been practicing law. When I graduated from Yale Law School in 1964, traditional labor law was all there was. Since then there has been an enormous growth of legal rights and responsibilities in the workplace, leading, of course to a lot more law work.

There's no one style that makes a successful labor lawyer. I think that, in general, you do have to have a certain amount of toughness, but toughness can be a lot different from smoking a cigar and pounding on the table. Toughness implies a keen intellect, an ability to win by any ethical means, and a willingness to withstand pressure when you properly analyze the situation and determine that it should be withstood. Perhaps the best training I've had for labor practice is playing a lot of poker. If you enjoy a good poker game and are good at it, you have a leg up on labor negotiations.

Practicing labor law is a wonderful way to earn a living because it's exciting. You really are in a constant succession of win or lose situations; union-organizing campaigns, arbitrations, negotiations, and court litigation. It's also very satisfying to be able to assist a large number of individuals who have to manage the destinies of employees; they are very appreciative when you are good at what you do and when you can communicate the knowledge that you have in a manner that is useful to them.

# PUBLIC INTEREST LAW

ublic interest lawyers use the power of legislation and the courts to benefit individuals or change society. They work in both the civil and criminal areas of law. Some specialize in work before specific administrative bodies. Others go to bat lobbying Congress for special interest groups. They advocate views covering the entire political spectrum, and the results of their work are evident in the front pages of our newspapers and in our everyday lives. Disarmament, the rights of the elderly, disabled, and children, prison reform, civil rights—these issues and thousands more are the concern of organizations that employ lawyers. Many of the most important cases of the century have been brought before the courts by public interest lawyers.

Public interest lawyers work in many settings. In the criminal area they work in public defender offices and associated backup centers. Civil practice includes legal aid offices and nonprofit lobbying groups. The attorney representing an elderly woman at a Social Security hearing and the one arguing a major impact class action suit before the United States Supreme Court are both practicing public interest law.

These are not the best of times for public interest lawyers. Politics and budget cuts have taken a heavy toll on many programs. Public funding has been drastically reduced. Many lawyers find themselves overburdened with cases. Compared to corporate and other fields of law, the pay is meager.

Given all the drawbacks, why would anyone choose a career in public interest law? The answers are as personal as the convictions of the attorneys themselves. In most job situations they trade high salaries for greater levels of independence, responsibility, client contact, and peer camaraderie. In no other area of law is there as great an opportunity to impact on people's lives. Public interest lawyers feel that they are doing something important with their skills.

Many would-be lawyers, in fact, enter law school with the idea of using the skills they gain to further a certain cause or assist those who might otherwise lack legal representation. Having the courage of one's convictions is critical to one's ability to cope with the day-to-day grind of public interest work. Public defenders, for instance, often handle 100 or more cases at a time. The overwhelming majority of these cases involve indigent clients, some of whom may not be convinced that the PD has their best interests at heart. Similarly, legal staffs of advocacy groups tend to be severely over-worked, and victories can easily seem few and far between.

For these reasons, perhaps, turnover in public interest law tends to be high, especially among legal aid lawyers and public defenders. For such attorneys, a loss in a courtroom means more than a slight corporate setback; it could mean that the client's life is forever altered, and in some cases shattered beyond repair.

Technological advances in information gathering and sharing have made public interest groups more interdependent and able to pool their expertise. Backup centers use computers to provide litigation support in complex cases in which a large volume of information is needed. Better information gathering processes make it easier for public interest groups and clearinghouse organizations to offer journals and conferences about cases and events.

This section will focus on the three major areas of public interest law:

◆ **LEGAL AID SERVICES**

◆ **PUBLIC DEFENDER OFFICES**

◆ **PUBLIC INTEREST GROUPS**

## JOB OUTLOOK

**JOB OPENINGS WILL GROW:** More slowly than average

**COMPETITION FOR JOBS:** Average

**NEW JOB OPPORTUNITIES:** Because of extensive cutbacks, the outlook in legal aid services is not rosy, but there is job turnover. Finding alternative funding sources (Howard University Law School administers the Reginald Heber Smith Community Lawyer Fellowship Program and VISTA also has some limited funding available) can improve your chances of landing a position. High turnover in public defender offices creates openings continually, even though the actual number of jobs will remain constant. Finding a position often depends on timing, so let the offices know you are available, and keep trying. More and more special interest groups are relying on the legal process to achieve their goals. New areas of law are being created as fast as court decisions are being handed down. Pinpointing interest groups before they become well-known can provide entree into the field.

## GEOGRAPHIC JOB INDEX

The Legal Services Corporation has offices in every state, as well as in Puerto Rico, the Virgin Islands, and Micronesia. LSC also has national resource centers that provide research and support to local programs. These are found in large metropolitan areas such as New York, NY, and Boston, MA. State and/or local governments may establish public defender offices, or they may purchase the services of legal aid lawyers for the defense of indigent defendants. Public interest groups exist in every state, and national resource centers are based in large metropolitan areas. National lobbying groups are usuallly located in Washington, DC, but can be found in other cities as well.

## WHO THE EMPLOYERS ARE

**LEGAL AID SERVICES** are provided by the Legal Services Corporation, a federal agency funded by congressional allocations and charged with making available free legal services to those who cannot afford to pay. The LSC has more than 250 offices nationwide and hires lawyers to represent indigent clients in civil cases. The Legal Aid Society, a private organization funded by contributions and grants, also provides free legal services nationwide.

**PUBLIC DEFENDER OFFICES** may be established by some state and local governments, but many contract with private groups to provide services in this area.

**PUBLIC INTEREST GROUPS** hire lawyers to advance their special interests through the legal process. These groups are privately funded through their sponsoring organizations. A few law firms also practice public interest law, but this work is largely supported by a healthy commercial practice.

## MAJOR EMPLOYERS

**LEGAL AID SERVICES**
The Legal Services Corporation, Washington, DC
Legal Aid Society, Independent branches nationwide.

**PUBLIC INTEREST GROUPS**
American Jewish Congress Commission on Law and Social Action, New York, NY
NAACP Legal Defense Education Fund, Inc., New York, NY
National Center for Youth Law, San Francisco, CA
National Center on Women and Family Law, Inc., New York, NY
New York Lawyers for the Public Interest, Inc., New York, NY
Sierra Club Legal Defense Fund, Washington, DC

## HOW TO BREAK INTO THE FIELD

Publications such as *The Directory of Legal Aid and Defender Services* can give you a line on where positions are available in legal aid and public defense. Enrolling in a clinical law program, supervised work experience while in law school, or a summer internship (these are almost always volunteer positions) can also be valuable in finding your first job in legal aid or public defense. For public interest groups, the best way to break in is an internship. Many organizations hire first- and second-year law students during the summer. This is an excellent way to gain exposure to the work and to make contacts that will be valuable after law school.

## INTERNATIONAL JOB OPPORTUNITIES

Legal aid offices in Puerto Rico, the Virgin Islands, and Micronesia do hire continental U.S. lawyers. There are no international opportunities in public defense. The United Nations hires a small number of attorneys to work on treaties and with its legal department on such issues as human rights, hunger, law of the sea, and space law. The competition for these positions is keen and preference is given to applicants from member nations other than the United States, which is already amply represented. Even so, most of the work is done in the New York, NY, headquarters, although some international travel may be involved.

# LEGAL AID SERVICES

Legal services lawyers represent indigent people in civil matters, such as family and divorce matters, child support cases, Social Security hearings, probate cases, traffic cases, landlord/tenant matters, and civil damage suits. Legal aid services are mostly dispensed through the federally funded Legal Services Corporation. Although it has come under attack in recent years, the agency has managed to survive through legal challenge and determination, but its funding—and hiring—has been greatly reduced. Consequently, workloads are heavy, and the pace of work is demanding. The same pressures are present in the Legal Aid Society, a private organization that receives some funds from the Legal Services Corporation and represents indigent people in civil, criminal, youth, and other legal matters.

## QUALIFICATIONS

**PERSONAL:** Desire to help the economically disadvantaged. An interest in the law as a means of social change. A strong belief in justice for all.

**PROFESSIONAL:** Ability to handle a demanding caseload and to work well under pressure. Ability to work independently without much direct supervision. Acceptance of the fact that the job seems never to be done.

## CAREER PATHS

| LEVEL | JOB TITLE | EXPERIENCE NEEDED |
|-------|-----------|-------------------|
| Entry | Lawyer | Law degree. Clinical law program or internship helpful |
| 2 | Administrator, local level | 3–5 years |
| 3 | Administrator, national level | 5+ years |

## JOB RESPONSIBILITIES ♦ ENTRY LEVEL

**THE BASICS:** Intake interviews with clients. Picking up the caseload of a colleague who has left. Telephone contact. Court appearances. (It is not unusual to find yourself in court from the beginning. The opportunity to gain lots of experience quickly is one of the major advantages of the job.)

**MORE CHALLENGING DUTIES:** Working and maintaining an increasingly large caseload. (Some attorneys juggle a hundred or more active cases at a time). More time spent in court.

## MOVING UP

There is the possibility of moving into supervisory or administrative positions. These would include directing a local or regional office and administering a national office or backup center.

# PUBLIC DEFENDER OFFICES

Every person charged with a criminal offense that involves the possibility of a prison term is entitled by law to be represented by an attorney. If a person cannot afford to hire an attorney, then the court must appoint one for him or her. Public defender offices provide lawyers for indigent criminal defendants. For the young criminal lawyer, this is the best place to gain invaluable courtroom experience quickly.

## QUALIFICATIONS

**PERSONAL:** A desire to work for the underdog. Tolerance for all types of people. Ability to listen with compassion. Capacity to be objective, not judgmental. A flair for the theatrical aspects of the courtroom. A willingness to be overworked and underpaid.

**PROFESSIONAL:** Strong research and courtroom skills. Ability to think on your feet. Ability to work independently.

## CAREER PATHS

| LEVEL | JOB TITLE | EXPERIENCE NEEDED |
|-------|-----------|-------------------|
| Entry | Lawyer | Law degree. Clerkship helpful |
| 2 | Administrator | 3–5 years |

## JOB RESPONSIBILITIES ◆ ENTRY LEVEL

**THE BASICS:** Handling motions, preliminary hearings, and trials. Court appearances. Some writing of briefs and appellate work.

**MORE CHALLENGING DUTIES:** More time in the courtroom. Larger caseload with more difficult cases.

## MOVING UP

A common career path is to establish your reputation as a trial attorney, then to move into supervisory and later administrative positions. Many administrators still maintain a caseload, although it is greatly reduced. Some move into backup or law reform positions, moving out of the intake level, and into more specialized representation. Others may shift into education and become clinical law instructors. The majority, however, use the experience gained in public defense to launch private practices.

# PUBLIC INTEREST GROUPS

Lawyers who work for public interest groups spend their time lobbying for their group's special interests, through legislative or judicial action, or high-impact test case litigation. In addition to funds raised by their sponsoring organizations, these groups are often supported by foundations and grants. Hundreds of such offices are involved in many specialized issues, and new specialties—genetic engineering, the definition of death, the rights of veterans—are growing rapidly in our fast-changing, complex society. The demand for positions with these groups is high, and experienced lawyers are given preference. This presents a challenge for the new graduate, but it does not mean that jobs are impossible to find. Showing an interest early in law school can help you make contacts and get you in the door.

## QUALIFICATIONS

**PERSONAL:** Commitment to a particular issue. A desire to help people and to effect change.

**PROFESSIONAL:** Excellent research and writing skills. Advocacy skills. Ability to speak well and comfortably in public.

## CAREER PATHS

| LEVEL | JOB TITLE | EXPERIENCE NEEDED |
|-------|-----------|-------------------|
| Entry | Lawyer | Law degree. Interest in a special issue. Internship experience helpful. |
| 2 | Administrator, local level | 3–5 years |
| 3 | Administrator, national level | 5+ years |

## JOB RESPONSIBILITIES ♦ ENTRY LEVEL

**THE BASICS:** Research, statistical compilation, and writing of briefs under the supervision of an experienced lawyer.

**MORE CHALLENGING DUTIES:** Independent work. Planning strategies for tackling issues. Determining what test cases to take on.

## MOVING UP

The most respected attorneys working for special interest groups earn prestige by becoming experts in their field. They contribute articles on their particular subject and speak at law schools and before other groups, and may become nationally or even internationally known for their work in their specialty.

# ADDITIONAL INFORMATION

## SALARIES

Money is not the reason people choose to work for a legal aid organization. Starting salaries average in the low $20,000s per year, and some positions start at less than $20,000. Administrators generally make from $30,000 to $40,000 per year; a select few national administrators may make more than $50,000 annually.

Entry-level salaries for public defenders also depend on the area of the country in which the job is located. Like legal aid lawyers, public defenders generally make much less than attorneys in private or corporate practice.

At public interest groups, average starting salaries are from $20,000 to $30,000 per year. Some of the more prestigious organizations pay more, but they usually look for attorneys who have some experience. Top legal salaries, however, can rise over $50,000.

## WORKING CONDITIONS

**HOURS:** Hours are long in all three areas, with an especially hectic pace in legal aid and public defense.

**ENVIRONMENT:** Although offices of a few of the more prestigious public interest groups may be well-appointed, don't expect much in the way of comfort in most public interest jobs. Most offices are designed for function, not form. Legal aid offices are often located in the neighborhoods of the people they serve. Because they must interview clients, attorneys may have a private office—or access to one—in some places.

**WORKSTYLE:** Legal aid lawyers spend much of their time interviewing clients, the rest defending them in civil procedures. Public defenders spend most of their day in court. Interviews are conducted in jails or police lockups. Public interest firms tend toward informality, with relaxed dress codes, because the principal function is not to impress clients. In all areas of public interest law the atmosphere is informal when compared to most private law practices; appearances are less important here, and there is less competition and more peer support than is generally found in private firms.

**TRAVEL:** Public interest groups may send attorneys to conferences and conventions, or to speak before various groups. Travel—except locally—is virtually nonexistent for public defenders and legal aid lawyers.

## INTERNSHIPS

Given the scarcity of jobs with public interest groups an internship can be invaluable in finding full-time employment. Law school placement services have information about available internships and the proper application processes. However, a little personal initiative in this area can go a long way. Join the group in which you are interested and volunteer your services to it while you are still in law school. If it does not offer formal internships, try to create one for yourself by pinpointing an area in which you can be useful and then offering to do the job.

## RECOMMENDED READING

### BOOKS

*Civil Rights Directory*, United States Commission on Civil Rights: revised periodically

*National Legal Aid and Defenders Association Directory of Legal Aid and Defender Services*, NLADA, National Legal Aid and Defenders Association: revised annually

*Nonprofit Counsel*, John Wiley & Sons: revised periodically

*State Information Book*, Infax Corp.: published biannually

*VLA Directory*, Volunteer Lawyers for the Arts: revised periodically

### PERIODICALS

*Cornerstone* (quarterly), National Legal Aid and Defenders Association, 1625 K Street, N.W., Washington, DC 20006

## PROFESSIONAL ASSOCIATIONS

National Legal Aid and Defenders Association
2100 M Street, N.W.
Suite 1601
Washington, DC 20037

# INTERVIEWS

### PUBLIC DEFENDER
### MICHIGAN

I was a classics major as an undergrad, then attended graduate school in English. Law seemed interesting to me so I took the LSAT. I graduated from the University of Michigan in 1977. In January of my senior year in law school a friend helped me get a clerking position at the public defender office. It was a very good way to start out. I learned about the job and the people who worked there. After my graduation, they offered me a job.

During my first year and a half to two years I was assigned to do misdemeanor cases. It was a fast pace, with many interesting clients and issues to deal with. It was a good way for an attorney to start out in criminal law. After that I moved into felony preliminary examinations, and eventually built up my caseload and began doing trials. I do all felony work now.

I meet a wide variety of people in my practice. That is what I like most about it. There are a tremendous number of stories, too. Just when I think I've heard them all along comes a new one. It's like a soap opera.

I do one or sometimes two trials a month. I'm pretty ambivalent about them. Trials can be very exciting, and there are frequent adrenalin rushes when you are in this competition. However, they are also stressful, because the focus is on you and there is so much at stake.

Much of my work involves negotiation with police, prosecutors, and judges. Most of our cases are resolved by plea bargaining. I think a public defender can get as good a deal, if not a better deal, than a privately retained lawyer could get. The people at the court know that they are going to have to work with me again tomorrow. I am in a much better position for my clients than a lawyer who is here on only one or two criminal cases per year.

This is a good job for a woman, and I would recommend it to others who are considering criminal law. At the beginning the major problems are with your clients. Many don't feel that a woman can take care of business. You find that attitude especially among some males. I counter that by being strictly professional and all business. The judges are more used to seeing women in the courtroom, and so there is not so much of a problem with them.

I pick up three or four new clients every week. I'm not able to do everything on my cases that I would like to do. The office used to have an investigator and a caseworker. Our present budget has eliminated those positions, so I do my own investigation and placement of clients into treatment programs.

We get paid well. Good benefits, too. Getting a paycheck is a big advantage to this job. I get a lot of support and advice from other people in the office. There is no other job where you can get as much experience in such a short amount of time as in a public defender office.

I see myself getting burned out on this job. Five years seems to be the turning point for most people. There is only so much human misery that you can take. I am looking around for other opportunities. After a while the faces and stories tend to blend into each other. When that happens, I realize it's time to think about moving on to something else.

**LOUIS GREGORY GONNELLA**
**SENIOR TRIAL ATTORNEY, ASSISTANT DEPUTY**
**PUBLIC DEFENDER**
**BERGEN COUNTY, NJ**

I have always been interested in criminal law. Prior to my present position I was engaged as a law clerk for the Criminal Division of the New Jersey Superior Courts in Essex County. At the conclusion of my clerkship I sent job applications to both the local prosecutor's office and the State Public Defender's central office in Trenton. The Public Defender's office circulated my application among the various county regions. I was interviewed by the Bergen County region about 11 years ago and hired in that same year.

The average caseload of a Public Defender varies between 100 to 120 cases at any given time. The position involves trial preparation, client interviews, researching, and various court appearances.

The major advantage of my career with the Public Defender's Office is the freedom of practice. A Public Defender handles his or her own caseload as he or she sees fit. There is no interference from one's superiors in this area. In essence, a Public Defender position is similar to a private practice that is exclusively criminal.

No position is ever exactly what you envision but, on the whole, the career I currently am engaged in is 90 percent of what I anticipated.

The criminal defense field, especially the Public Defender's Office is stimulating and exciting. I do not anticipate leaving in the foreseeable future.


**MARC STERN**
**CO-DIRECTOR, LEGAL DEPARTMENT**
**AMERICAN JEWISH CONGRESS**
**NEW YORK, NY**

I attended Yeshiva College and Columbia Law School. I also did a clerkship at the Court of Appeals. I was never the political type in school, but I had no taste for corporate practice. A friend in my legal drafting class told me about a summer internship position at the American Jewish Congress. That was how I started, and I have now been here 12 years.

The Commission on Law and Social Action as a public interest law firm was an innovative idea when it was first formed after World

War II by a group of lawyers. There was considerable discrimination against Jews, many times in the form of a gentleman's agreement not to hire them. After the war, most minority groups were no longer willing to put up with second class citizenship. The office began preparing friend of the court briefs for the civil rights cases which were then being brought. In the 1950s we were instrumental in immigration law reform.

I like this job because I am always learning something new. I also do a lot of lobbying of other Jewish organizations, and some public speaking. I do a great deal of reading and library work. I have to become familiar with many areas of law as issues arise. I also write opinion letters, speak to reporters, and participate in academic symposia. We use the services of many volunteer lawyers, and we also have summer associates to help with the research.

Our day is pretty much nine to five. I answer many telephone calls requesting information from all over the country. Most just want to know if a particular action is legal. They want to know if they have legitimate reason to be upset at something, and if anything should be done about it. I may step in and contact administrators or other officials and indicate our opinion of the law as it applies to a particular action. Many times just calling their attention to a particular Supreme Court decision will be enough to correct a situation.

Through my work I have become an expert in the area of church–state relations. I advise local counsel involved in cases and provide them with research and briefs. The office has been involved in litigation touching most of the issues in this area.

The whole area of public interest litigation has become more challenging as more conservative groups have set up their own public interest law firms. In the past liberal groups were practically alone in their approach, but now there are a great number of conservative groups on the other side of the issues.

This job allows me to be involved in the most pressing issues of the day. I do a lot of reading, prepare academic papers, and write magazine articles.

I have a strong personal commitment to what we do here, and I think that commitment is necessary in public interest law. It is a thrill to open a newspaper and see an article about some issue or case that I've been involved in. Not many lawyers get that kind of reinforcement.

# STATE AND LOCAL GOVERNMENT

P racticing law for state and local governments can be both a satisfying and a stimulating career choice. Government attorneys are important public servants dedicated to improving the public welfare and preserving the integrity of our judicial system. Government cases often raise challenging legal questions of constitutional dimension, as well as interesting procedural problems. The work requires an attorney who can think analytically, speak and write effectively, and research thoroughly.

Government offices offer a stable, structured environment with a full range of criminal and civil cases. Many such offices have training programs and provide individualized supervision for new attorneys. At the same time, both new and experienced attorneys are often allowed considerable autonomy in handling cases. These positions are generally ones in which attorneys can continue to develop, to learn about new aspects of practice, and to refine important lawyering skills.

The challenges and rewards for working at the state and local level vary greatly by region. In major cities, of course, prosecuting and civil attorneys can expect to have heavy case loads. In areas with low population densities, work may not be as taxing. Regions that have a great amount of business and commerce activity will keep civil attorneys more than busy, while lawyers in district attorneys' offices in high-crime areas face a never-ending torrent of cases.

Many small towns appoint attorneys who work almost on a retainer basis. Usually, these lawyers hold regular positions in private or sole-proprietor firms. They work for the local government on a part-time, as needed basis. Many times, such positions are a stepping stone to a career in politics.

Turnover rates in state and local government tend to be high. Many new attorneys use these slots as springboards to more lucrative careers in private practice. The high turnover, of course, is good news for aspiring state and local government attorneys. Many district attorneys' offices are on a constant lookout for new, enthusiastic talent.

# CRIMINAL PROSECUTION

Prosecuting attorneys bear an important responsibility in helping to protect society and, at the same time, in assuring that accused persons are given fair and impartial treatment within the criminal justice system. Their work, although involving exclusively criminal law, is varied and demanding. It requires both an understanding of the procedures governing the trial of criminal matters and a knowledge of state or local statutory law and court precedents.

Criminal practice of this nature entails frequent appearances in court, before either a judge or a jury, to argue the legal questions that have arisen and finally to present evidence in the trial of the case. Similarly, criminal lawyers are often called on to prepare a variety of different pleadings, such as indictments (the accusatory instruments that initiate cases), and papers; every question of law or procedure, such as a motion to suppress evidence and exclude it from the trial, may require the submission of a brief or memorandum by the attorneys in the case. In addition, the work in a district attorney's office involves a range of other important decisions, including determining the validity of arrest procedures, assessing the factual merits of an investigation, and deciding whether to pursue a matter to trial or to bargain for a guilty plea.

In the course of practice, a prosecuting attorney comes into continual contact with other law enforcement officers, with defense attorneys, with often distraught victims, with witnesses whose attitudes vary from outrage to apathy, and with criminals and alleged criminals. It is a practice that involves important questions and compelling issues that can seriously affect the lives of the people involved. In all these contexts, a district attorney is an advocate for the people. As such, the person in this position requires tact, sensitivity, and a high degree of commitment.

## JOB OUTLOOK

**JOB OPENINGS WILL GROW:** About as fast as average

**COMPETITION FOR JOBS:** Strong

The competition for prosecutorial jobs is getting more intense each year as other areas of practice become more difficult to enter. Good grades and honors in law school are playing an increasingly important role in hiring.

**NEW JOB OPPORTUNITIES:** The future of most prosecutors' offices seems secure. Unfortunately, crimes are committed every day everywhere in the country and the government needs to maintain a staff of attorneys to handle the resulting cases. In areas with particularly high or increasing crime rates, there will generally be some pressure to add more attorneys to the prosecutor's staff to deal with court congestion and case backlogs. At the same time, remember that prosecutors' offices are part of local governments and as such may be subject to certain budget constraints in determining raises and staffing increases, especially during times of fiscal difficulties.

## GEOGRAPHIC JOB INDEX

Most cities and counties throughout the country have prosecutors' offices. The sizes of these offices range from one or a few attorneys in small towns to hundreds of attorneys in a major city like New York, NY.

## WHO THE EMPLOYERS ARE

Most crimes are prosecuted by the district attorney's office for the city or county. In addition, in some areas, the criminal prosecution of juvenile crime may be handled by another governmental agency or body. On the state level, the attorney general's office may have a few divisions that handle particular criminal investigations or other penological issues. These offices, if they exist, are generally smaller or more specialized than the district attorney's office. For example, some divisions may handle both the civil and criminal prosecution of environmental issues or certain fraudulent transactions.

## HOW TO BREAK INTO THE FIELD

Law students interested in criminal prosecutorial careers should take as many related course offerings as possible—criminal law, criminal procedure, constitutional law, and evidence are essential. District attorney's offices look quite favorably on students who participate in a clinical program, particularly if it is a criminal clinic, because these students will have the experience handling actual cases. For the same reason, students should seek summer or part-time employment with a prosecutor's office or some other criminal litigation office during law school. Those individuals who do not begin working in a prosecutor's office immediately after graduation are more likely to secure later employment with such an organization if they have practiced with another criminal law office, for example, private criminal practice, or have engaged in som form of litigation.

Many of the larger prosecutors' offices conduct interviews on law school campuses in the fall for permanent positions beginning the following year. In New York, NY, for example, four of the five borough offices conduct such interviews. Students who do not obtain an on-campus interview or who wish to apply to an office that does not have such recruitment efforts should send a résumé and cover letter to the personnel office, the attorney in charge of hiring, or the first assistant district attorney. Hiring is usually done only after a complete interview, and sometimes more than one interview. Because there will be many graduates applying for similar positions, contacts in the field can be instrumental. The more people who know you and are favorably impressed with you, the greater the likelihood that you will be given an interview. Obviously, how well you handle the interview will often determine whether you are offered a position.

## THE WORK

Most district attorney's offices are divided into different divisions. Some offices assign each division responsibility for a different stage of the criminal proceeding: hearings, trials, motions, and appeals, for example. Attorneys in these divisions handle a wide range of cases at the same stage of development. Other offices are divided into divisions that handle specific kinds of cases, such as narcotics, homicides, major felonies, and misdemeanors. Either method of dividing an office gives attorneys the opportunity to develop an expertise in the kinds of issues involved in their cases. Small offices may simply assign cases as they are filed, without reference to any particular division of labor or expertise.

## QUALIFICATIONS

**PERSONAL:** Assertive. Interested in working for the public. Capable of withstanding time pressure. Ability to be confronted daily with the consequences of criminal brutality. In general, a willingness to live within the city limits.

**PROFESSIONAL:** Well-spoken. Organized, prepared, and decisive. Knowledgeable about criminal law.

## CAREER PATHS

Some attorneys choose to do prosecutorial work for most of their careers and others leave the district attorney's office after several years. The litigation experience acquired in a prosecutor's office provides an excellent background for any other litigation or criminal justice position. Many attorneys apply the experience they have gained to the private practice of law.

## JOB RESPONSIBILITIES ◆ ENTRY LEVEL

**THE BASICS:** Some offices will assign new attorneys to the less glamorous tasks, such as case assessment—an examination of cases as they arise to determine their trial-worthiness—or preliminary hearing—an early trial stage in which evidence is presented. This is viewed as a training opportunity; a chance to see how cases are built and to develop needed practice skills in a less demanding context.

**MORE CHALLENGING DUTIES:** After an initial period, most attorneys are responsible for trying cases. Each attorney is expected to handle all aspects of a case, including dealing with witnesses, researching legal issues, writing briefs, planning strategy, and appearing in court. Generally, supervisors and other attorneys in the office are available to discuss the various issues and problems that arise in any case.

## MOVING UP

Advancement in a prosecutor's office usually follows one of two patterns. Attorneys can become supervisors or administrators in a particular division or in a central division. In such positions, they may retain responsibility for handling specific cases as well as acquire additional responsibility for overseeing the work of junior attorneys and planning the work of the office. Alternatively, some experienced attorneys may advance by moving to a more prestigious or challenging division, such as homicide.

## SALARIES

As in other areas of employment, starting salaries for attorneys in state and local government vary by region. In most areas of the nation, starting salaries range from $22,000 to $30,000 per year. In large cities like New York and Los Angeles, starting salaries may reach close to $40,000 for some positions. Cost of living increases as well as yearly step increases or credit for experience are common. In smaller cities, wages are slightly lower. For the most part, prosecutorial work pays reasonably well for the public sector, although certainly less than is paid by the private sector.

## WORKING CONDITIONS

**HOURS:** Eight-hour work days are a minimum; hours will often exceed that. In practice, it is necessary to devote as many hours as are required to complete all aspects of each case properly. Courts impose deadlines on criminal cases which must be met even if that means staying late and working weekends. Obviously, the more familiar an attorney becomes with issues and practice, the less time certain tasks will take. However, being a prosecutor is never an easy job, and demands on your time can be great when a case is being readied for trial.

**ENVIRONMENT:** Most prosecutors' offices are located in a municipal building of some sort. Although the actual physical environment may vary, it is unlikely that a prosecutor's office will be luxurious. Much of the attorneys' time is also spent in the criminal court buildings.

**WORKSTYLE:** The pace of litigation is often dictated by the rules of the courts and the timetables set by particular judges. Preparing for a trial is often hectic. The periods between trials are generally devoted to factual investigations, legal research, and writing.

**TRAVEL:** There is little chance for travel in these positions.

## INTERNSHIPS

Many of the larger prosecutors' offices have summer internship programs for students, as well as part-time positions during the school year. For second-year students, these are frequently paid positions. Many offices begin accepting applications and interviewing applicants as early as the preceding fall. The large offices often conduct interviews on the law school campuses in the fall for their summer positions. Your law school placement office will have details about application processes and interview appointments. Small district attorney's offices may not advertise available positions, and students should contact those offices themselves to determine availability of positions and the application process.

# CIVIL LAW

Civil law includes a broad range of subjects dealing with every kind of legal issue other than criminal matters. Real estate, banking, securities, labor, tax, trusts, and estates are some of the specialty areas of civil practice. Civil attorneys perform a wide variety of functions: preparing documents such as contracts and wills, negotiating the terms of agreements, providing advice on business matters, interpreting statutes, or pursuing disputed cases in court. Regardless of the particular issues under consideration, a civil attorney must have a full grasp of the law in the area, including any court rules of civil procedure, and a good command of such legal skills as research, writing, and oral advocacy.

Working for a state or local government can be an exciting way to practice civil law. State and municipal governments, perhaps more than any private organization, because of their size and the number of services they provide, need attorneys in almost every specialty area of civil law. Housing, transportation, welfare, mental health, and family services are examples of government services, each of which is governed by its own body of law. Attorneys are essential to the provision of these services and to the resolution of a variety of other problems and questions, including construction contracts, employee disputes, environmental issues, and financial arrangements.

Working as an attorney for a government office often means handling cases that affect the lives of many people and involve substantial sums of money. Such work affords the opportunity to come into contact with some of the area's finest private lawyers and with a variety of public officials. In addition, it offers attorneys the power to marshal the resources of the state or city to effect public improvements.

## JOB OUTLOOK

**JOB OPENINGS WILL GROW:** About as fast as average

**COMPETITION FOR JOBS:** Keen

Competition for government jobs on both the state and local levels is becoming more intense. Although opportunities still exist, high grades, honors, and previous legal experience are all important factors in obtaining employment. Some of the more prestigious government offices even impose special requirements on applicants, for example, that they have practiced law for a stated number of years, before they will be considered.

**NEW JOB OPPORTUNITIES:** Most states and cities have a large staff of attorneys who handle civil matters. As attorneys leave these government positions, they are usually replaced. Therefore, there are openings in these offices on a fairly frequent basis. However, as part of the government, these law offices are also subject to a variety of budget restraints that sometimes limit the number of new positions that are created and that sometimes force vacated positions to be "frozen" or unfilled for a period of time.

## GEOGRAPHIC JOB INDEX

Most state positions are located in the state capitals, although several states with small capitals also have law offices in the state's major city or cities. Pennsylvania has most of its offices in Harrisburg and some additional offices in Philadelphia and Pittsburgh; New York has state law offices in both Albany and New York City.

Almost all cities, counties, and even some smaller towns have their own civil attorneys.

## WHO THE EMPLOYERS ARE

On a state level, the largest law offices are generally those of the attorney general. In addition, most state agencies, commissions, boards, and executive and legislative offices have legal staffs. Similarly, on a local level, the major law office in any city is that of the corporation counsel or city solicitor. In addition, local agencies and commissions also maintain legal staffs. The mayor's office and other leading city executives or legislators generally hire a number of attorneys.

## HOW TO BREAK INTO THE FIELD

Some attorneys general, city solicitors, and agency offices will interview on law school campuses in the fall for positions that begin after graduation the following year. Others may list openings with law schools as they become available. There are, however, many state and city agencies that never contact law schools but do hire attorneys at different times throughout the year. The best approach is to send a résumé and cover letter directly to each agency or office that interests you and then to follow up with a phone call to determine whether any positions exist and the status of your application. Remember that many government civil law offices, both state and local, are controlled by civil service laws.

This means that at least some agencies are not allowed to hire attorneys on a permanent basis unless they are on an approved civil service list. Law students and graduates interested in government careers should be careful to take the civil service exams when they are offered so that they can be ranked on the approved lists. Courses in municipal law and administrative law, as well as experience in litigation or in a government office, are helpful for individuals seeking employment in this field.

## THE WORK

Most attorney general's offices and city solicitor's offices have a number of different divisions, each responsible for different areas of practice, such as litigation, administrative law, and appeals, or for cases of a particular nature, such as environmental law, human services, and finance. Cases include those brought against the government as well as those brought by the government. In most instances, attorneys in these offices represent one or more state or city agencies in the exercise of their authority. The state and city agencies also have their own legal staffs that handle much of their civil work. The nature of the legal work varies with the agency; some attorneys work as hearing examiners, others become involved in the day-to-day legal issues of the agency, such as challenges regarding individual entitlements to agency benefits. The various executive staffs and the staffs of the different state and city commissions and boards exist to provide legal advice on all relevant matters and to handle any required legal transactions.

## QUALIFICATIONS

**PERSONAL:** Ability to deal effectively with others. Reliable. Dedi-. cated. Ability to manage time well. Interest in public issues.

**PROFESSIONAL:** Good communication skills. Careful attention to details. Knowledge of civil law and procedure.

## CAREER PATHS

Working for either an attorney general's or a city solicitor's office is an excellent career opportunity. Practicing law in either office prepares an attorney for most other civil law jobs. These offices are generally well respected by the private sector, and many attorneys are able to secure positions with firms and corporations if they leave the government. Although the nature of the practice in a state or city agency is not as varied, working there also offers considerable civil law experience. Attorneys in these agencies often go on to other government positions, with the attorney general, for example, or to private practice.

## JOB RESPONSIBILITIES ♦ ENTRY LEVEL

THE BASICS: Beginning attorneys should expect to be assigned a number of less complex cases from which they can learn the basic elements of legal practice; some may be asked to co-counsel a case with a more experienced attorney. Depending on the size of the office and its caseload as well as on the attorney's ability and initiative, even a new attorney may be given considerable responsibility for more difficult cases.

MORE CHALLENGING DUTIES: More experienced attorneys will have more varied caseloads and will be given more responsibility and autonomy in handling those cases. In addition to handling cases, government attorneys may be called on to write opinions about proposed agency or legislative action, to work on legislation, or to resolve administrative questions.

## MOVING UP

Most attorneys who remain in government service advance by assuming supervisory or administrative positions. Others move to different divisions or agencies.

## SALARIES

Positions with an attorney general or city solicitor are generally well paying, as far as government jobs go. For instance, city attorneys in San Antonio, TX, start with an annual salary of about $30,000. Again, attorneys for larger cities start out at higher salaries. Positions with state agencies generally pay a little less, but almost all government attorneys receive excellent benefits and regular salary increases.

## WORKING CONDITIONS

**HOURS:** Most government attorneys have sizable caseloads, each with their own court deadlines. Such attorneys are, in general, free to manage their own time. However, in meeting case responsibilities, they may be required at times to work long hours or to work on weekends.

**ENVIRONMENT:** Government attorneys often work in state office and municipal buildings. These are frequently older buildings where the emphasis is on practicality. In some instances, government offices occupy more modern space in a private building. The New York state attorney general's office, for example, is located in the World Trade Center in New York, NY.

**WORKSTYLE:** An attorney's time is essentially divided among doing legal and factual research, dealing with opposing counsel, writing, and making appearances in court. Legal research is generally conducted in the law library, while factual research may involve dealing with witnesses, reviewing documents, or working with the office's investigative staff. Meetings with and telephone calls to opposing counsel are essential to the progress of every case. Writing briefs, motions, opinions, and correspondence consumes a considerable portion of the day. The number and length of court appearances will vary from occasional brief status conferences to trials that can last several weeks.

**TRAVEL:** State attorneys may be required to travel on occasion to some other city in the state. Travel outside the state is unlikely. Similarly, city attorneys are not likely to travel, except on those rare instances where a case is being argued in a court outside the local jurisdiction.

## INTERNSHIPS

Many attorney general's and city solicitor's offices have summer internship programs for students and accept part-time student interns during the school year. Certain agencies also may hire student assistants. Most positions are for second-year students; some are voluntary, others carry a stipend. Fewer positions exist for first-year law students, and these are generally voluntary.

## RECOMMENDED READING

### BOOKS

*Biennial Report*, National Association of Attorneys General: 1988

*National Directory of Prosecuting Attorneys*, National District Attorneys Association: 1988

## PROFESSIONAL ASSOCIATIONS

National Association of Attorneys General
444 North Capitol Street, N.W.
Suite 403
Washington, DC 20001

National District Attorneys Association
708 Pendleton Street
Alexandria, Virginia 22134

# INTERVIEWS

**LUIS R. GARCIA**
**ATTORNEY FOR THE CITY OF SAN ANTONIO**
**SAN ANTONIO, TX**

I started my law career nearly 40 years ago. For the past 15 years, I've worked for the city of San Antonio. Prior to that, I had my own private practice. In my private practice, I did a little of everything—criminal law, probate, administrative, and so on. Today, lawyers tend to be more specialized. Specialization has become a necessary part of law practice. The law grows ever more complex, and there are more courts and more lawyers than ever.

I had several reasons for leaving my private practice to work for the city. First, I had the opportunity to come in at the top level of the administration. I was always interested in the public sector—as a private attorney, I had done a great deal of pro bono work. I figured that by taking the job, I'd help the city as well as help myself earn a living.

Our organization is responsible for prosecuting civil and criminal cases to enforce city ordinances. We also prosecute Class C misdemeanors for the state of Texas. As you can imagine, there are plenty of such cases in a city the size of San Antonio. In fact, we handle about 300,000 cases a year—more than all other jurisdictions of Bexar County combined.

We do this work with a relatively small staff. The city has about three dozen or so attorneys working for it. I have eight attorneys in my department. My main job is to administer my office. I assign cases to the other attorneys in my department. I take on very few cases myself.

It's a fact of life that salaries in the public sector just can't match what the private sector has to offer. We hire people right out of law school who are interested in working in the public sector. The work we do provides new lawyers with a great deal of solid, practical training. The attorneys who started in our organization and have gone on to private practice have been very successful.

**ALEXANDER P. WAUGH, JR.**
**COUNSEL TO THE ATTORNEY GENERAL OF NEW JERSEY,**
**ASSISTANT ATTORNEY GENERAL**
**TRENTON, NJ**

I was in private practice with two firms for a total of ten years and also served as Assistant Counsel to the (New Jersey) Governor for two years before becoming an Assistant Attorney General.

I had been contacted by the Attorney General and asked if I would be interested in leaving private practice. For me, this was an opportunity to be involved in government service again at the policy-making level.

The Attorney General in New Jersey has authority over a wide variety of areas—criminal law, of course, but also representing and advising almost every agency of State government, including the State Police. Because of this, the issues I face on the job are not limited to criminal law.

My day usually runs from 8:00 to 6:30 and involves reviewing state government activities, meeting with the Attorney General or other people on his behalf, and writing briefs and memos. Because of my private practice background, I am also becoming involved in handling individual cases.

I expect to return to private practice eventually.

# TEACHING

aw teaching is a career for individuals who get satisfaction from seeing others develop as thinkers and doers, and who enjoy in-depth questioning of issues and the stimulation generated by exploring various perspectives on a subject. Those who enter the field have a fascination with the philosophy of the law and a strong scholastic interest in writing, research, and the exchange of ideas.

Most lawyers come to teaching after several years in private practice or high-level government service. Most law school teachers start their teaching careers in their 30s. Often they have prestigious clerkships behind them. There are no hard and fast requirements for advanced degrees as there are for teaching other disciplines at the graduate level. All law teachers hold a law degree (J.D.) and some hold an LL.M. (master of legal letters), especially those who specialize in a particular area, such as tax. This degree may be earned with one year of full-time study. The J.S.D. (doctor of juridical science) degree is the legal profession's equivalent of the Ph.D., and is held only by those whose concerns are purely academic. Few who pursue a J.S.D. ever practice or intend to practice law.

Teaching offers more flexibility in terms of time than any other area of law. During the academic year teachers give two courses per term, summers are "free." However, this seemingly light schedule is deceptive. A professor teaching a course for the first time can expect to put in 20 to 30 hours per week in preparation time. Several hours per week are devoted to meeting with students and reading and grading papers and exams. The demands to pursue scholarly work are great; faculty are expected to publish the results of their research and to stay current with developments in several areas of the law. They also serve administrative functions on school committees.

Entry into the profession is extremely competitive; however, teaching opportunities in law schools can also be found on an adjunct (part-time) basis. In addition, individuals interested in teaching law-related courses may find employment in business schools, undergraduate political science and history departments, and paralegal institutes.

## JOB OUTLOOK

**JOB OPENINGS WILL GROW:** About as fast as average

**COMPETITION FOR JOBS:** Keen

The number of law teaching positions depends largely on law school enrollment. During the 1970s, legal education was in a period of expansion, which resulted in a 50 percent increase in full-time law faculty. But enrollment at law schools decreased during the 1980s, which has led to a corresponding drop in the number of law teaching opportunities and an increase in competition for a limited number of positions.

It is difficult to precisely assess the supply/demand ratio of law teaching candidates to available positions for several reasons. First, although some schools announce their anticipated openings widely, others do so selectively by apprising certain deans or faculty members at other schools. Second, law faculty candidates inform schools of their teaching interests through a variety of sources, making a determination of the actual number of applicants quite difficult. Third, because there is no mechanism for certification among law faculty, other than graduation from law school, there is no centralized office that can measure the potential number of applicants entering the marketplace.

**NEW JOB OPPORTUNITIES:** As new areas of the law emerge, such as computer law and environmental law, there has been an increase in the number of specialized course offerings and, therefore, a need for qualified individuals to teach these subjects. This growth in diversified course offering, however, will be coupled with more practitioners entering the teaching profession, increasing the competition for jobs.

## GEOGRAPHIC JOB INDEX

Law schools are located throughout the United States, but the following states have the greatest number of law schools accredited by the American Bar Association:

| | |
|---|---|
| California | 16 |
| New York | 14 |
| Ohio | 9 |
| Illinois | 9 |
| Texas | 8 |
| Massachusetts | 7 |
| Pennsylvania | 6 |
| Michigan | 5 |
| Virginia | 5 |
| Washington, DC | 5 |

Candidates are encouraged to be geographically flexible when starting their careers in order to maximize the number of teaching options.

## WHO THE EMPLOYERS ARE

**LAW SCHOOLS** provide the majority of law teaching positions. There are 175 American Bar Association-accredited law schools in the United States.

**BUSINESS SCHOOLS** training M.B.A.s offer students courses in business law, contracts, tax, and labor relations.

**UNDERGRADUATE SCHOOLS** offer law-related courses through the political science and history departments.

**PARALEGAL SCHOOLS** train legal assistants in the basics of law practice.

## HOW TO BREAK INTO THE FIELD

There are a variety of ways to find a law teaching job. They include:

**FACULTY APPOINTMENTS REGISTER:** The Association of American Law Schools (AALS) compiles a register of all candidates interested in law teaching or law school administration. Each candidate completes a standardized application that is circulated to all law schools for evaluation. Candidates in whom there is interest are contacted for an interview at the AALS faculty recruitment conference (see below).

**AALS PLACEMENT BULLETIN:** Published six times during the academic year, contains announcements of available teaching and administrative positions throughout the country. It is available on a subscription basis or through most law school placement offices.

**AALS FACULTY RECRUITMENT CONFERENCE:** Candidates who submit applications to the AALS faculty and administrative registers as well as those who send for positions announced in the *AALS Placement Bulletin* and who pass initial screening are then interviewed at the annual AALS faculty recruitment conference. The conference, usually held in early December, is attended by most ABA-accredited schools, as well as hundreds of job applicants. Following an evaluation of the candidates by the faculty selection committees, the most promising candidates are invited to individual campuses for more extensive interviewing.

**REFERRALS:** The aforementioned methods of establishing contact between candidates and schools notwithstanding, referrals still play an important part in the law faculty hiring process. A dean or faculty member may make inquiries on behalf of an exceptionally promising graduate student or former student. In addition, graduate law program directors also contact law schools in an effort to assist their J.S.D. and LL.M. graduate students.

**RÉSUMÉ MAIL CAMPAIGN:** Because only a limited number of law teaching positions are advertised through the *AALS Placement Bulletin*, the *Chronicle of Higher Education*, and the *American Bar Association Journal*, it is advisable to contact schools in which you are particularly interested by sending a résumé and cover letter that includes the names of references to the chairperson of the faculty personnel committee. In cases where the name of the chairperson is unknown, send your letter to the dean's office, and it will be forwarded accordingly.

**ON-CAMPUS INTERVIEWS:** Some faculty personnel committees send a representative to selected law schools to interview LL.M. and J.S.D. candidates as well as strong third-year J.D. students. These visits are usually coordinated by the placement office. Candidates should contact the office in September to apprise the placement office of their teaching interests and to find out the schedule for on-campus interviews.

**ADJUNCT POSITIONS:** Schools offer numerous courses that may be taught by legal practitioners on a part-time basis. Teaching in this capacity gives the school an opportunity to observe one's pedagogical skills and scholarly pursuits. It also gives the candidate an opportunity to evaluate his or her performance in the classroom before making a commitment to a full-time teaching career.

## INTERNATIONAL JOB OPPORTUNITIES

Overseas teaching positions are extremely rare, even for experienced, tenured faculty. The few positions available to teachers who wish to spend their sabbatical year at a foreign university are coordinated through a visiting faculty register compiled by the AALS.

# THE WORK

## QUALIFICATIONS

**PERSONAL:** Self-confidence. Commitment to legal education and working with students. Enjoyment of working and interacting with scholastic peers.

**PROFESSIONAL:** Law degree from well-respected law school and class rank in the upper 10 to 20 percent. Member of law review or publication in other legal journals. Advanced degrees (LL.M. or J.S.D.) helpful. Judicial clerkship helpful. Experience in private or corporate practice or in government service. Other helpful credentials: faculty research assistant, instructor in a legal writing or clinical law program, success in moot court or client counseling competition.

## CAREER PATHS

| LEVEL | JOB TITLE | EXPERIENCE NEEDED |
|-------|-----------|-------------------|
| Entry | Instructor | Law school degree |
| 2 | Assistant professor | 0–3 years |
| 3 | Associate professor | 3–7 years |
| 4 | Professor | 7–10 years |

## JOB RESPONSIBILITIES ♦ ENTRY LEVEL

THE BASICS: Preparing for and teaching basic courses. Meeting with students. Scholarly research and writing. Serving on school committees.

MORE CHALLENGING DUTIES: Teaching more specialized courses, or courses of your own design. Chairing school committees. Continued pursuit of greater scholarly achievement.

## MOVING UP

Reaching the academic goal of full tenure will be achieved both through evaluation from students and through the quality of your research. How frequently and where you publish the findings of your research will play a great part in your movement up the academic ladder. Tenure is granted by a committee usually made up of the deans and full professors, who will take all aspects of your academic performance into account. The faculty needs and the structure of the school will also affect your attainment of this important academic distinction. In general, tenure review begins after the fifth year of teaching, by which point you will have been named a professor. A sabbatical is taken during the sixth year to concentrate on scholarly research. If tenure is not granted at the end of this year, the teacher is expected to seek employment elsewhere. Few teachers remain on the faculty of an institution after tenure has been denied.

# ADDITIONAL INFORMATION

## SALARIES

Law teaching salaries vary according to the size and reputation of the law schools. Larger and better known law schools tend to pay higher salaries. In the late '80s, the average salaries for law school teachers ranged from about $27,000 per year for instructors, to nearly $45,000 per year for associate professors and $62,000 per year for full professors. Those same positions in non-law disciplines paid about $23,000, $35,000, and $45,000, respectively. Law faculty have the opportunity to supplement their income by writing casebooks (textbooks describing cases in law with the writer's commentary on them); "of counsel" relationships with private law firms or corporations, and consultancies.

## WORKING CONDITIONS

**HOURS:** Junior faculty can expect to spend 20 to 30 hours per course in preparation time in addition to time spent teaching, evaluating coursework, serving on school and professional committees, meeting with students, and doing scholarly research and writing. Senior faculty members may spend less time on course preparation; however, they may become more involved in administrative functions.

**ENVIRONMENT:** Faculty members usually have their own offices within the law school.

**WORKSTYLE:** Depending on the location and characteristics of the particular law school involved, workstyles can vary greatly. Generally, law teaching provides an opportunity for self-starters who are well-disciplined to schedule and regulate their own output.

**TRAVEL:** The amount of travel one does as a law teacher depends on how active one is on professional society committees which meet in various locations. Faculty members may also travel to serve as counsel to private firms, corporations, or the government, or to guest lecture at other law schools.

## RECOMMENDED READING

**BOOKS**
*Directory of Law Teachers*, Association of American Law Schools: revised annually

**PERIODICALS**

*The American Lawyer* (monthly), Am-Law Publishing Corporation, New York, NY

*Journal of Legal Education* (quarterly), Association of American Law Schools, Washington, DC

*Legal Times* (weekly), Prentice-Hall Law & Business, Englewood Cliffs, NJ

*Student Lawyer* (monthly), American Bar Association, Chicago, IL

## PROFESSIONAL ASSOCIATIONS

American Academy of Judicial Education
2025 L Street, N.W.
Suite 903
Washington, DC 20006

American Bar Association
Section of Legal Education and Admissions to the Bar
1155 East 60th Street
Chicago, IL 60637

Association of American Law Schools
One Dupont Circle, N.W.
Suite 370
Washington, DC 20036

Society of American Law Teachers
President: Wendy W. Williams
Georgetown University Law Center
600 New Jersey Avenue, N.W.
Washington, DC 20001

# INTERVIEWS

JOHN SEXTON
DEAN
NEW YORK UNIVERSITY SCHOOL OF LAW
NEW YORK, NY

Although my career path to law teaching was somewhat circuitous, law was always part of my master plan. Events conspired to cause me to fall in love with teaching. During my freshman year in college, I began teaching history and coaching the debate team at an all-girls high school in Brooklyn. It was through that debate team that I caught the teaching bug. The students were like family, and I was their teacher for four intensive years. Our team competitions took us to tournaments throughout the country, and each visit was supplemented with an exploration of the community and its cultural events. We raised money to support the team activities through folk and rock concerts. When our monetary needs increased, I developed the John Sexton LSAT (Law School Admissions Test) preparation course, which enabled us to raise significantly more money. Along the way, for my own stimulation and financial support, I completed a Ph.D. in comparative religions at Fordham University and became a tenured faculty member and Chairperson of the Theology Department at St. Francis College in Brooklyn.

In 1972 I turned 30, decided it was time to get my legal career under way, and began to wind down my coaching responsibilities. I attended Harvard and loved the study of law so much that I took a year off between years one and two so I could read more and prolong the experience. During my second year, I had the opportunity to teach a class in civil procedure to 120 first-year students while the professor was out of town. The next year, I did a repeat two-week performance with several members of the Harvard faculty observing me. This helped my career greatly, because they were able to speak on my behalf when I began to look for a teaching position.

I had one additional detour on my path to teaching law. I spent two years in Washington, DC, as a judicial clerk to Judges Leventhal and Bazelon of the U.S. Court of Appeals and with Chief Justice Burger—a terrific experience, and one that created bonds that exist to this day.

In 1981, I joined the faculty at NYU. I taught the basic civil procedure course to first-year students, as well as a first-year elective course. I also taught a seminar on religion and the Constitution to third-year students. A couple of years ago, I became Dean of the law school.

The teaching life is stimulating indeed, and I find that working with students really keeps me young. I make sure to spend time with my family, and I try to balance that with the demands of my work.

### Susan Bryant
### Assistant Dean for Student Affairs
### Southern Methodist University School of Law
### Dallas, TX

In the four years that I've been out of law school, I've learned one fundamental lesson: A career in law can involve a lot more than lawyering.

I went to law school with a specific goal in mind. I wanted to work with people who have mental health and legal problems. Actually, my interest in helping emotionally troubled people came before my interest in the law. I had already earned a Master of Arts in psychology before I entered the Georgetown University Law Center in Washington, DC.

When I graduated from Georgetown, I looked for a position in a public interest organization in the Washington area, but I didn't find anything in that competitive job market. I took a position as a staff attorney with the Legal Services Corp. in its Colorado Springs, CO, office for about two years. Legal Services is a congressionally funded program that serves indigent clients in civil matters.

The work at Legal Services was exciting and personally rewarding, but my decision to marry precipitated relocating in the Dallas area. When the position at the SMU School of Law was offered to me, I accepted it. I wouldn't say that my two years with Legal Services helped prepare me for my job at SMU, but it did give me the practical legal experience that's needed to help guide students more effectively.

As assistant dean for student affairs at the law school, my main responsibilities are in the areas of admission, financial aid, and student counseling. Obviously, this is a far cry from what I had envisioned for myself when I entered law school. When I counsel students about career paths, I sometimes use myself as an example of the diversity that a law degree offers. At Georgetown, I was in a study group of five women; we all ended up picking very different legal careers. I've found that the original direction you set for yourself sometimes doesn't happen, but there are always other opportunities along the way.

# ENTREPRENEURIAL OPPORTUNITIES IN LAW

The fact that there are more than 175,000 private law firms in the United States is testament to the entrepreneurial opportunities available to legal professionals. Most of the nation's private firms are classified as being small—that is, they have fewer than 25 attorneys. Many of these firms are made up of five or fewer attorneys, and sole proprietorships are also common.

Experts say, however, that times are getting tough for small law firms. Two trends do not bode well for these firms. First, more and more businesses are moving away from private counsel and are building their own in-house legal departments. Second, the very large firms—the megafirms—are starting to dominate the legal business. The National Association for Law Placement projects that by the year 2000, the institutional lawyer—the lawyer who works for a megafirm—is likely to be the predominant form of practitioner in the legal profession.

As megafirms and in-house legal departments grow, the job shortage that has made the market so tough for law school graduates will begin to ease. Not only will there be more jobs available, but also the number of law school graduates has leveled off since the glut days of the late 1970s and has declined slightly in the past few years. The job market will continue to be highly competitive, especially for the lucrative positions offered by the large firms. Still, fewer attorneys may choose an entrepreneurial path when high paying, stable positions are available.

Clearly, in most cases smaller firms don't have the resources to compete against the big guns for important clients. Size, however, isn't always the determining factor in getting and keeping clients.

Despite trends toward ever larger megafirms and massive corporate legal departments, there will always be a place for the small firm in the American legal system. "Storefront" law firms, which are usually run by sole proprietors, will continue to be of service to clients who don't require a lawyer's services often. Beyond the storefront attorney, the growth of small-business proprietors in America should spur demand for legal services. Small-business clients often opt for representation by small firms as they tend to be apprehensive about large firms for fear of being lost in the shuffle.

Experts say that lawyers who have specialized in a business aspect of law will stand a better chance of succeeding in setting up their own firm. Three business aspects of law stand out as being in greater demand in the coming years: tax law, real estate law, and patent law. Of the three, tax lawyers will probably enjoy the most success in sole-practitioner firms. Tax laws seem to be in constant change; as a result, most small businesses need expert tax advice to comply with state and federal laws.

Of course, few are able make to the leap from law school directly into their own practice. Most attorneys entertain the thought of going into business for themselves only after they have spent a number of years honing their skills while working for others. Indeed, that experience often dictates the type of work an attorney chooses when embarking on a solo career. Lawyers who cut their teeth prosecuting criminal cases in a district attorney's office, for instance, are more likely to set up as criminal law practitioners.

An attorney who decides to "go solo" has to be prepared to do more than lawyering. After all, a sole-practitioner firm is also a small-business venture. Going solo means taking on the responsibilities of finance manager, office manager, personnel director, go fer—whatever it takes to keep a business going. It may mean taking a few minutes' break from preparing a case to go shopping for some office equipment or to call the stationery story to order some needed supplies.

For most attorneys who decide to make a go of it on their own, the first few years are the most challenging to get through. Not only does one have to work hard to develop a base of clients and establish credibility, but one also has to run a tight ship and make do without a lot of the amenities that attorneys in larger firms take for granted. But for those who manage to pull through those first years and establish thriving practices, the rewards are plentiful: complete control of one's destiny, a sense of accomplishment, and a base from which to build for the future.

Although setting up an independent firm is the most obvious entrepreneurial path an attorney can take, it isn't the only one. Many lawyers have used their legal careers as springboards into other endeavors. In some cases, attorneys become immersed in a particular business or aspect of business and find themselves drawn more to the world of commerce than to the law. In recent years, this has been particularly true in the real estate trade. A number of prominent developers began their careers as practicing attorneys.

Attorneys have also registered entrepreneurial successes in the publishing industry. Law & Business, now a part of the Simon & Schuster publishing empire, was started by a couple of attorneys who identified a market need for directories of attorneys and proceeded to fill that need. Brownstone Publishers in New York is another venture started by a lawyer. Brownstone publishes newsletters and guides for real estate developers and investors covering various aspects of real estate law. And, of course, dozens of lawyers have hit the shelves in the nation's bookstores with various guides and advice books geared toward legal laymen.

Business and publishing are but two of the career paths that some attorneys have taken out of the courtroom. Such nonlegal paths run the gamut, from representation of athletes to ownership of sports franchises, from legal consultants to major corporations to advocates of consumers rights. A career in law need not begin and end in the courtroom; it can be as wide-ranging as an individual's ideals and aspirations.

## RECOMMENDED READING

### BOOKS
*Building the Dynamic Law Practice*, by Arnold S. Goldstein et al, John Wiley & Sons: 1987

*Flying Solo: A Survival Guide for the Solo Lawyer*, American Bar Association: 1984

*How to Build a Successful Estate Practice*, by Robert S. Hunter, Lawyers Co-operative Publishing Co.: 1986

*How to Get and Keep Clients*, by Jay G. Foonberg, Lawyers Alert: 1986

*How to Start and Build a Law Practice*, by Jay G. Foonberg, American Bar Association, 1986

*Marketing Your Practice*, by Austin G. Anderson, American Bar Association: 1986

# BIBLIOGRAPHY

### DIRECTORIES
*American Lawyer Guide to Law Firms*, Steven Brill, ed., Am-Law Publishing Corp.: revised annually

*Career Opportunities in Communications Law*, Federal Communications Bar Association: 1982

*Directory of Bar Associations*, American Bar Association: revised annually

*Directory of Intellectual Property Lawyers*, Lynn LoPucki, ed., Clark Boardman Co., 1988

*Directory of Legal Aid and Defender Offices in the U.S.*, J. Cornell, B. Sanders, and D. Sher, eds., National Legal Aid Defenders Association: revised annually

*Directory of Legal Employers*, National Association of Law Placement: revised periodically

*Employment Opportunity Survey of Government Agencies*, by Marilyn Norton, National Association for Law Placement: revised annually

*Federal and State Judicial Clerkship Directory*, National Association of Law Placement, revised periodically

*Internships in Federal and State Government*, The Graduate Group: revised annually

*Law & Business Directory of Bankruptcy Attorneys*, Lynn LoPucki and Ann T. Reilly, eds., Prentice-Hall Law & Business: 1988

*Law & Business Directory of Corporate Counsel*, Prentice-Hall Law & Business: revised annually

*Law and Legal Information Directory*, Gale Research Co.: revised biannually

*Lawyer's Register by Specialties and Fields of Law*, Margaret A. Schultz, ed., Jury Verdict Research Inc.: revised biannually

*Legal Careers in Business*, Penny J. Parker, ed., National Association for Law Placement: 1984

*Martindale-Hubbell Law Directory*, Martindale-Hubbell, Inc.: revised annually

*NALP Membership Directory*, National Association for Law Placement: revised annually

*New Hiring: Government Jobs for Lawyers*, Moira K. Griffin, ed., American Bar Association Law Student Division: 1984

*Parker Directory of Attorneys*, Parker & Son: revised annually

*VLA Directory*, Volunteer Lawyers for the Arts: revised periodically

*Want's Federal-State Court Directory*, Want Publishing Co.: revised annually

*Who's Who in American Law*, Marquis Who's Who: revised biannually

**GENERAL REFERENCE**
*The Best Lawyers in America*, by Steven Naifeh and Gregory White, Seaview/Putnam: 1983

*Blacks in the Law: Philadelphia and the Nation*, by G. R. Segal, University of Pennsylvania Press: 1982

*Building the Dynamic Law Practice*, by Arnold S. Goldstein et al, John Wiley & Sons: 1987

*Chicago Lawyers: The Social Structure of the Bar*, by John P. Heinz and Edward O. Laumann, American Bar Foundation: 1983

*Employment Report and Salary Survey*, National Association for Law Placement: revised annually

*Flying Solo: A Survival Guide for the Solo Lawyer*, American Bar Association: 1984

*From Law Student to Lawyer*, by Gary A. Munneke, American Bar Association: 1984

*Guide to Federal Jobs*, Resource Directories: revised periodically

*How to Build a Successful Estate Practice*, by Robert S. Hunter, Lawyers Co-operative Publishing Co.: 1986

*How to Get and Keep Clients*, by Jay G. Foonberg, Lawyers Alert: 1986

*How to Start and Build a Law Practice*, by Jay G. Foonberg, American Bar Association: 1986

*Law Students: How to Get a Job When There Aren't Any*, by William T. Carey, Carolina Academic Press: 1986

*The Lawyers*, by Martin Mayer, Greenwood Press: 1980

*Lions in the Street: The Inside Story of the Great Wall Street Law Firms*, by Paul Hoffman, Saturday Review Press: 1973

*Lions of the Eighties: The Inside Story of the Powerhouse Law Firms*, by Paul Hoffman, Doubleday & Co.: 1982

*Marketing Your Practice*, by Austin G. Anderson, American Bar Association: 1986

*The Million Dollar Lawyers*, by Joseph C. Goulden, Berkeley Publishing Co.: 1981

*Nonlegal Careers for Lawyers: In the Private Sector*, American Bar Association: revised periodically

*Nonprofit Counsel*, John Wiley & Sons: revised periodically

*The Partners: Inside America's Most Powerful Law Firms*, by James B. Stewart, Simon & Schuster: 1983

*The Prosecutors: Inside the Offices of the Government's Most Powerful Lawyers*, by James B. Stewart, Simon & Schuster: 1987

*Stating Your Case: How to Interview for a Job as a Lawyer*, by Joseph Ryan, West Publishing Co.: 1982

*The Tenth Justice: The Solicitor General and the Rule of Law*, by Lincoln Caplan, Alfred A. Knopf: 1987

*The Washington Want Ads: A Guide to Legal Careers in the Federal Government*, Moira K. Griffin, ed., American Bar Association: revised annually

*What Color Is Your Parachute? A Practical Manual for Job Hunters and Career Changers*, by Richard N. Bolles, Ten Speed Press: revised periodically

*Where Do I Go from Here? A Career Planning Manual for Lawyers*, American Bar Association: 1972

*Women Lawyers: Perspectives on Success*, Emily Couric, Prentice-Hall Law & Business: 1984

*Your New Lawyer: The Legal Employer's Guide to Recruitment, Development and Management*, by Gary A. Munneke and the American Bar Association, American Bar Association: 1983

**PERIODICALS**
*American Corporate Counsel Association Docket* (bimonthly), American Corporate Counsel Association, Washington, DC

*The American Lawyer* (monthly), Am-Law Publishing Corp., New York, NY

*Cornerstone* (quarterly), National Legal Aid and Defenders Association, Washington, DC

*International Lawyers Newsletter* (bimonthly), Washington, DC

*JD/MBA Quarterly* (quarterly), National Association of JD/MBA Professionals, Indianapolis, IN

*Journal of Legal Education* (quarterly), Association of American Law Schools, Washington, DC

*Legal Times* (weekly), Prentice-Hall Law & Business, Englewood Cliffs, NJ

*National Association for Law Placement Notes* (monthly), NALP Administrative Office, New Orleans, LA

*National Law Journal* (weekly), New York, NY

*National Legal Employment Report*, The Federal and National Legal Employment Report, Washington, DC

*Of Counsel* (biweekly), Prentice-Hall Law & Business, Englewood Cliffs, NJ

*Public Interest Employment Report* (biweekly), Public Interest Clearinghouse, San Francisco, CA

*Student Lawyer* (monthly), American Bar Association, Chicago, IL

# NOTES